Learning Language Arts Through Literature

THE GRAY

TEACHER BOOK

By

Diane Welch and Susan Simpson

Common Sense Press
™

The *Learning Language Arts Through Literature* series:

The Blue Book - 1st Grade Skills
The Red Book - 2nd Grade Skills
The Yellow Book - 3rd Grade Skills
The Orange Book - 4th Grade Skills
The Purple Book - 5th Grade Skills
The Tan Book - 6th Grade Skills
The Green Book - 7th-8th Grade Skills
The Gray Book - 8th-9th Grade Skills
The Gold Book - High School Skills

ISBN 1-880892-88-X

Introduction

As parents we watched and marveled at the way our little ones learned to talk. By listening and responding to English spoken well, they were able to communicate quite clearly. The process was so gradual that they were not even aware it was taking place.

It is the belief of those associated with the *Learning Language Arts Through Literature* series that written language can best be learned in the same manner. By reading fine literature and working with good models of writing, children will receive a quality education in language arts. If you desire to teach using this integrated approach to language, this curriculum is for you.

Dr. Ruth Beechick has confirmed that this method of teaching is an appropriate and successful way to introduce our young students to the joys of reading, writing, and thinking. Our own experiences using these lessons with children have encouraged us to share them with you. Their enjoyment and enthusiasm for reading and writing is an unmatched recommendation for this method of teaching.

The **integrated language approach** has the benefits of all teaching methods. By working with pieces of real literature, you focus on grammar, vocabulary, writing, reading, spelling, penmanship, and thinking skills. Your student has the best advantage for learning skills in this effective and lasting manner.

Grammar is taught in conjunction with writing, not as an isolated subject. Your student's **vocabulary** will be enhanced by reading the good literature which has been carefully chosen for his grade level. A study of prefixes, suffixes, and roots will also aid your student to higher understanding. We realize that every student functions at different reading levels. For the more hesitant reader, we recommend more read aloud time with your student. Grade appropriate **reading skills** are included. Your student will review basic **spelling rules** using misspelled words from his daily writing and the *Commonly Misspelled Words List*. **Thinking skills** are developed throughout the activities in this manual. Anytime a student is asked to respond to the literature with discussion, writing, drawing, or completing an activity, your student is developing his thinking skills.

How to Use This Book

This book will help you teach your student language art skills. It provides you with materials and suggestions that will be an encouragement and benefit to you as you create a learning environment.

The Gray Book is intended for use after *The Green Book* of the *Learning Language Arts Through Literature* series. The lessons in *The Green Book* utilize a unit study approach to language arts, while *The Gray Book* is largely based on dictation lessons. As in the other books in this series, we have made an effort to use fine literature whenever possible to serve as a model for your student.

Dictation Lessons

Twenty-three of the lessons are based upon literature passages to be dictated to your student. Before dictating, read the entire passage to the student while he listens only. Instruct him to listen for sentence endings, questions, and quotations. Begin the dictation exercise by reading one sentence at a time. If necessary, repeat the sentence, reading one phrase at a time. The student's work should be double spaced to make the editing process easier, as well as to give room for further work with the passage. If your student has difficulty with dictation, allow him to copy the passages for several lessons and then try dictating again.

In addition to taking the passage from dictation, instruction will be given throughout the week which covers such topics as punctuation, capitalization, parts of speech, grammar, creative writing, etc. In most lessons the student will take a spelling test covering words from the most *Commonly Misspelled Words List* found in the *Appendix*. Also, your student will increase his spelling skills as he learns to list mispelled words in his *Personal Spelling List*. He may create his own list or use the one provided in the *Student Activity Book*. Finally, most lessons include a *Vocabulary Builder* exercise using selected words from the passage.

Review Activities

After most dictation lessons you will find optional *Review Activities* to reinforce the material covered during the week.

Assessments

Four *Assessments* are included throughout the year for evaluating your student's progress.

Book Studies

Approximately every eight weeks your student will have a two week literature lesson based upon a selected book. After reading the book, the student will review vocabulary words and learn to interpret word meaning from understanding its content. He may also choose from a variety of suggested activities that will expand his understanding of what he has read as well as his writing and thinking skills. The four required books are listed in the *Materials to Use* on the next page.

Writing Unit

Finally, four lessons make up a special writing unit that covers five weeks. In this unit your student will develop his writing skills by completing a narrative paper, a persuasive paper, a compare and contrast paper, and a research paper.

Note to Teachers

Some of the writing assignments your student will be asked to complete in this book may seem very hard. It cannot be emphasized enough that the writing process takes time. Be sure to give your student plenty of time to complete an assignment. Help him by spending time talking about the assignment and how he will write it. Encourage him to work on a rough draft, editing and rewriting as he thinks through the assignment. All writers must go through this process of ordering and reordering their thoughts, so be encouraging and patient as your student learns to think and write well.

In closing, be creative in finding ways your student can share his writing. You will be surprised how this will motivate the student to write more and better. Seek out relatives, neighbors, and friends who will give positive encouragement to the budding author. Also, many students enjoy being involved in a "literary club" with other home-educated students. Poetry, stories, and other writing may be read aloud and studied together.

 Enrichment Activities

In most lessons you will find the treasure chest icon for the *Enrichment Activities*. This is your cue to look for the activity located in the *Student Activity Book* where they are listed in full.

Answers to these activities are found in the back of this manual. While optional, these activities develop reasoning skills necessary for higher level learning.

Skills Index

The *Skills Index* is located in the back of the manual. To ensure that the skills commonly held appropriate for eighth to ninth grade instruction were adequately covered, much research was involved in the writing of this book. This information was primarily gleaned from:

You CAN Teach Your Child Successfully by Ruth Beechick

If your student has a particularly strong or weak area, you can easily locate those skills using the *Skills Index*. If your student receives standardized testing, skills listed on the test may also be found here.

Materials To Use

This program is designed to be easy to use. The only materials necessary are:
1. A loose-leaf notebook with paper, pen or pencil, and highlighter.
2. Reference materials: thesaurus, dictionary, and Bible.
3. The books needed for the *Book Studies* may be found under various publishers. Page number referrals are based upon the following publishers.

    Across Five Aprils by Irene Hunt; Follett Publishing Co.
    A Lantern in Her Hand by Bess Streeter Aldrich; Penguin Group
    Eric Liddell by Catherine Swift; Bethany House
    God's Smuggler by Brother Andrew; Penguin Group

You may purchase these books at your local or Christian bookstore, or you may check them out from your library.

Student Activity Book

A *Student Activity Book* is available for your student. Daily exercises corresponding to each lesson are included for easy use.

Table of Contents

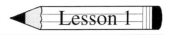

Everywhere Washington wore an air of expectancy. The hillocks of lumber, which had been piled for weeks along the Avenue, had finally been fashioned into grandstand and bleachers. Every street corner was garnished with the navy blue of District policemen. The gray lampposts were decorated with small American flags and pictures of Truman and Barkley. Red, white, and blue bunting was everywhere. In a few hours, forty thousand marchers and more than forty floats would form a column seven miles long in honor of the President of the United States. It was Inauguration Day, January 20, 1949.

A Man Called Peter by Catherine Marshall
(Used by permission, Chosen Books)

1. a. Take this literature passage from dictation. Compare your copy with the model and make corrections.

   b. Note that the words *Avenue* and *Disctrict* are capitalized. These words are usually not capitalized unless they are part of a particular avenue or district. Why do you think the author capitalized these words? We will be studying capitalization tomorrow.

   c. Briefly, who were Truman and Barkley? If you don't know, look in the encyclopedia under Harry Truman and Alben Barkley.

2. a. The building blocks of any piece of writing are words. A good writer must not only choose the right words to convey his thoughts, but the words also need to be spelled correctly. Even though spelling seems easy for some and difficult for others, anyone can learn to be a better speller by practicing. In each lesson you will have the opportunity to practice spelling. Read the following suggestions to attack your spelling problems.

✎ **Teacher's Note: As your student completes each lesson, choose skills from the *Review Activities* that he needs. The *Review Activities* follow each lesson.**

1.
b. *Avenue* is capitalized because the author is referring to a particular avenue, Pennsylvania Avenue. *District* is capitalized because the author is referring to the District of Columbia.

c. Harry Truman was the 33rd president of the United States. He first became president when President Franklin D. Roosevelt died early in his fourth term. Truman finished the term and then was elected to serve again from 1949-1953.

Senator Alben W. Barkley of Kentucky was chosen to run with Truman for the vice-presidency in 1948.

How to Attack your Spelling Problems

1) Keep a List
   Each week, your teacher will give you ten words from the *Commonly Misspelled Words List* in the *Appendix* at the back of the book. Add any misspelled words to the *Personal Spelling List* found in the *Appendix* in the *Student Activity Book*. Or create your own *Personal Spelling List* on a separate piece of paper. Next, add any words you misspell in your weekly dictation to your list. Add any misspelled words from any other writing you do during the week.

2) Analyze your Mistakes
   Ask yourself the following questions:

   Are there mistakes that you make in spelling rules?
   Ex: believe (**i** before **e** except after **c**)

   Are there words where you omitted silent syllables or letters?
   Ex: guard

   Are there words you misspelled because you mispronounced them?
   Ex: *liberry* instead of *library*

   Are there words where you used wrong letters because they sound like other letters?
   Ex: necessary

   Are there words that are not spelled the way they sound?
   Ex: bouquet

   Did you use double letters correctly?
   Ex: occurrence

   Did you add prefixes and suffixes correctly?
   Ex: mis + spell = misspell   love + able = lovable

   Did you write one word when you meant another?
   Ex: *desert* instead of *dessert*

3) Practice Spelling by Syllables
   Many long words are spelled just as they sound.
   Breaking a word into syllables will help you spell it.
   Ex: in / cred / i / ble

4) Use Correct Pronunciation
   Many spelling errors are made because words are
   mispronounced.
   Ex: *athalete* instead of *athlete*; *goverment* instead of
        government

5) Use a Dictionary
   It might be easier to guess, but make it a habit to look up
   words you are not sure about.

6) Spelling Rules
   Although there are exceptions to most spelling rules,
   learning a few basic rules can be helpful. Turn to the
   Appendix at the back of the book for a list of basic
   Spelling Rules.

b. Your teacher will give you a spelling test using the first ten
   words from the *Commonly Misspelled Words List*. Add
   any words you miss to your *Personal Spelling List*. Add
   any words you missed in the literature passage to this list
   and study the list. Be prepared to take a test at the end of the
   week.

c. You will remember that **nouns** name persons, places, things,
   or ideas.
   Ex: girl, park, swing, happiness

   These are all **common nouns** because they do not name a
   particular person, place, thing, or idea. Common nouns are
   not capitalized.

   A noun that names a particular person, place, thing, or idea
   is called a **proper noun**.
   Ex: Mary, New York, Pepsi

2.

c. Washington, Avenue, District, American, Truman, Barkley, President, United States, Inauguration Day, January

d. l) *Everywhere, The, Every, The, Red, In, It*
Capitalize the first word in every sentence.

2) *Washington, Avenue, District, United States, Truman, Barkley, President, Inauguration Day, January*
Capitalize all proper nouns.

3) *American*
Capitalize all proper adjectives.

3.

a. lumber; Avenue; Red, white, and blue; hours; Inauguration Day; January 20

b. Commas are used to set off the date when it is renaming a day (Inauguration Day) Commas are used to separate the day and the year (January 20, 1949)

c. Red, white, and blue bunting was everywhere.

d. which had been piled or weeks along the Avenue
The sentence still makes sense.

✐ **Teacher's Note:** A clause is a group of words which has a subject and predicate; a clause may be independent or dependent. See Lesson 4, 2d.

The words *Avenue* and *District* in the literature passage are capitalized because they are referring to a particular avenue and district, although the author doesn't use the whole name.

Underline all the proper nouns in the literature passage.

d. We can observe certain patterns or rules by studying the words that are capitalized. For example, a capital letter is used at the beginning of the first word in each sentence.
Ex: The hillocks of lumber.....
Underline the first word of each sentence.

There is one more capitalized word that is not underlined. Underline this word and try writing a capitalization rule for this word. If you do not know, review the *Capitalization Rules* in the *Appendix* at the back of the book.

e. Review the *Capitalization Rules* in the *Appendix* at the back of the book.

3. a. Just as you used your powers of observation to review capitalization rules yesterday, today you will review some rules for the use of commas. Circle the commas in the literature passage.

b. Explain the use of the commas in the last sentence. If you do not know, review the *Comma Rules* in the *Appendix* at the back of the book.

c. Which sentence is an example of the rule to use commas to separate words in a series?

d. The second sentence beginning "The hillocks of" contains a parenthetical phrase. A **parenthetical phrase** is a word or phrase that interrupts the flow of the sentence and could be omitted without changing the meaning of the sentence.

Commas are used to set off a parenthetical phrase. Circle the parenthetical phrase in the second sentence. Read the sentence omitting this phrase. Does the sentence still make sense?

e. There is one more comma used in this literature passage. The comma is used to separate the introductory phrase from the rest of the sentence. An **introductory phrase** is a phrase at the beginning of a sentence which, when removed, still makes sense. The phrase introduces the sentence by adding more information such as telling how, when, or why.

Ex: After the game, everyone went out for pizza.

After the game is the introductory phrase.

Find the introductory phrase in the literature passage and circle it.

f. Add correct capitalization and commas to these sentences.
1) last night mary bathed her little lamb.
2) the lamb always followed mary when she went to church the park or wal-mart.
3) even though he knew better the lamb followed her to school one day.
4) it was on the last day before easter april 14 1988.
5) using the lamb as a visual aid mrs. goodlady the second grade teacher taught the class about jesus.

g. Review the *Comma Rules* in the *Appendix* at the back of the book.

4. a. The literature passage for this week describes a scene that took place on January 20, 1949. The purpose of description is to help the reader see, hear, or in some way experience something. To which sense does Mrs. Marshall's description appeal? She does this by vividly telling us what the scene looks like.

b. Today you will write a **descriptive paragraph**. You may choose one of the following topics or use one of your own. Remember to use words that appeal to one of our senses: sight, smell, hearing, taste, or touch.
    ♦ Sunday dinner at your house
    ♦ backstage just before the curtain goes up
    ♦ sitting on a beach watching the sunrise
    ♦ the view from the top of a lighthouse

3.
e. In a few hours

f.
1) Last night, Mary bathed her little lamb.
2) The lamb always followed Mary when she went to church, the park, or Wal-Mart.
3) Even though he knew better, the lamb followed her to school one day.
4) It was on the last day before Easter, April 14, 1988.
5) Using the lamb as a visual aid, Mrs. Goodlady, the 2nd grade teacher, taught the class about Jesus.

4.
a. sense of sight

5. a. Optional: On a separate piece of paper, rewrite the literature passage from dictation. Pay special attention to capitalization and commas.

   b. Take a spelling test using the words you missed this week.

   c. Write another descriptive paragraph appealing to a different sense than you chose yesterday.

   d. Choose skills from the *Review Activities* on the next page.

Review Activities

Choose skills your student needs to review.

1. *Spelling Rules*
   Review the *Spelling Rules* found in the *Appendix* at the back of the book.

2. *Proper Nouns and Commas*
   Copy the following paragraph taken from *A Man Called Peter*, capitalizing the proper nouns and inserting commas as needed.

   At this juncture james broadbent a cousin who had emigrated to the united states came back to scotland on a visit. Though jim had arrived at ellis island with even less than the minimum amount of money required by the immigration authorities he had subsequently been most successful in america. He was an engineer for the m. w. kellogg company in new york. He had made a quick trip over to scotland from swansea wales where he was doing a job for the anglo-iranian oil company.

3. *Parenthetical Phrase*
   Underline the parenthetical phrase in the paragraph.

4. *Introductory Phrase*
   Put parentheses around the two introductory phrases in the paragraph.

2. At this juncture, James Broadbent, a cousin who had emigrated to the United States, came back to Scotland on a visit. Though Jim had arrived at Ellis Island with even less than the minimum amount of money required by the immigration authorities, he had subsequently been most successful in America. He was an engineer for the M. W. Kellogg Company in New York. He had made a quick trip to Scotland from Swansea, Wales, where he was doing a job for the Anglo-Iranian Oil Company.

3. a cousin who had emigrated to the United States

4. At this juncture
   Though Jim had arrived at Ellis Island with even less than the minimum amount of money required by the immigration authorities

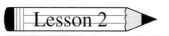

Teacher's Note: As your student completes each lesson, choose skills from the Review Activities that he needs. The Review Activities follow each lesson.

Jesus replied and said, "A certain man was going down from Jerusalem to Jericho; and he fell among robbers, and they stripped him and beat him, and went off leaving him half dead. And by chance a certain priest was going down on that road, and when he saw him, he passed by on the other side. And likewise a Levite also, when he came to the place and saw him, passed by on the other side. But a certain Samaritan, who was on a journey, came upon him; and when he saw him, he felt compassion."

Luke l0:30-33 (NASB)

1. a. Write the literature passage from dictation. Correct any errors. Add any words you misspell to your *Personal Spelling List*.

   b. Take a spelling test using the next ten words from the *Commonly Misspelled Words List*. Add the ones you miss to your *Personal Spelling List* and study them throughout the week.

   c. You effortlessly build your vocabulary each day by one simple activity: reading. Without looking up an unfamiliar word you often figure out its meaning by how it is used in the sentence or the **context**. An author will sometimes help you by restating the word in a different way, giving you examples of the word, or by comparing or contrasting the word in the sentence. Below are examples of each of these methods:

      1) Restating: He gave the impression that he was *infallible*, incapable of making mistakes. (*Infallible* means incapable of making mistakes.)
      2) Examples: This week's spelling lesson taught how to correctly add *suffixes*, such as **-ing**, **-ed**, and **-s**, to root words. (*Suffixes* are letters added to the end of a word.)
      3) Comparing: Her *kinetic* behavior reminded me of an old fashion pinball machine. (*Kinetic* means pertaining to motion.)

4) Contrasting: Even though *fatigued*, he somehow found the strength to finish his race. (*Fatigued* means tired.)

Another way to build your vocabulary is by becoming familiar with word parts. Two word parts are prefixes and suffixes. **Prefixes** are added to the beginning of root words and **suffixes** are added to the end. **Root words** are words used to form other words. Knowing the meaning of word parts can help you analyze unfamiliar words.

d. Vocabulary Builder

Philia is a Greek word meaning love or friendship. If you knew the word parts *anthropos* (man), *logos* (word), and *Angli* (English), you could figure out the meanings of these words:

- philanthropist - one who cares about his fellow man
- philologist - one who loves words
- Anglophile - one who loves England

You will find the *Word Parts Lists* in the *Appendix*. They contain three helpful charts: *Prefixes*, *Suffixes*, and *Roots*.

You may have played the game called "Fictionary" or "Dictionary," where an unfamiliar word is chosen and the players make up dictionary sounding definitions and try to guess which is the correct one. To help build your vocabulary, you will be doing something like this with words taken from your dictation exercises.

Using the context clues along with what you already know, write a dictionary sounding definition for the word *compassion*. If you need a little more help, look at the *Word Parts Lists* in the *Appendix*. You will see that the prefix *com* is Latin meaning *with* or *together*. Now look up the word in the *Glossary* provided in the *Appendix*. How well did you do? Write a sentence using this word to show you understand the meaning. You will be using this exercise to learn new words throughout this book.

2.

a. (he) a certain man
   (they) robbers
   (him) a certain man
   (him) a certain man
   (him) a certain man
   (that) the road from
       Jerusalem to Jericho
   (he) a certain priest
   (him) a certain man
   (he) a certain priest
   (he) a Levite
   (him) a certain man
   (who) a certain Samaritan
   (him) a certain man
   (he) a certain Samaritan
   (him) a certain man
   (he) a certain Samaritan

✎ Teacher's Note: *Who* is a relative pronoun. *That* is a demonstrative pronoun. Do not expect your student to find these pronouns. Interrogative, relative, and demonstrative pronouns are discussed in 2e.

2. a. Language would be very awkward if we always had to use a noun to refer to a person, place, thing, or idea. **Pronouns** (*pro* meaning *for*) are useful because they can be used in place of a noun to name a person, place, thing, or idea. The noun to which the pronoun refers is called the **antecedent**.

For example, in the literature passage, pronouns are used fifteen times. Without them the first sentence would read:

> Jesus replied and said, "A certain man was going down from Jerusalem to Jericho; and the certain man fell among robbers, and the robbers stripped the certain man and beat the certain man and went off leaving the certain man half dead."

Circle the pronouns and underline their antecedents in the remaining sentences of the literature passage. Finish reading the literature passage using the antecedents instead of the pronouns.

b. Among the pronouns you circled were the words *he, him,* and *they*. These are called personal pronouns because they take the place of nouns that name persons or objects. Personal pronouns may indicate number: **singular** or **plural**. They can also indicate person: **first person** (the person speaking), **second person** (the person being spoken to), and **third person** (the person being spoken about).

PERSONAL PRONOUNS

Singular	Subjective	Possessive	Objective
1st person	I	my, mine	me
2nd person	you	your, yours	you
3rd person	he, she, it	his, her, hers, its	him, her, it

Plural	Subjective	Possessive	Objective
1st person	we	our, ours	us
2nd person	you	your, yours	you
3rd person	they	their, theirs	them

c. Complete this chart using the pronouns *he*, *him*, and *they*. Write if the pronoun is in the first, second, or third person; and if it is singular or plural.

	Person	**Number**
Ex: we	first	plural
he		
him		
they		

d. Pronouns can also show possession. The cloak belonging to John would be *John's cloak*. This is a **possessive noun**. By using a **possessive pronoun**, we would say *his cloak*. Possessive pronouns also can indicate number and person.

Rewrite the following sentences using the correct possessive pronouns for the possessive nouns.
1) Julie forgot *Julie's* lunch.
2) Bill said he would share *Bill's* lunch.
3) This was an example of *Julie and Bill's* friendship.

Although we are used to using an **apostrophe** (') to indicate possession, possessive pronouns do not need apostrophes.

Ex: Julie's lunch   -   her lunch
      cat's tail   -   its tail

The most common mistake is to use *it's* instead of *its* as a possessive pronoun. *It's* is the contraction for *it is*.

Hint
Possessive pronouns do not use apostrophes.

2.

c.

	Person	Number
he	3rd	singular
him	3rd	singular
they	3rd	plural

d. 1) Julie forgot *her* lunch.
2) Bill said he would share *his* lunch.
3) This was an example of *their* friendship.

e. There are two other kinds of pronouns used in the literature passage: *who* and *that*. The pronoun *who* may act as an interrogative pronoun when it is used to ask a question such as "Who will be going to the camp?"

Interrogative Pronouns
who   whose   whom
which   what

However, in the literature passage, *who* is used as a relative pronoun. These pronouns are used to relate the phrase, "who was on the journey" to another phrase, "a certain Samaritan." *Who, whose, whom, which,* and *what* are used also as relative pronouns.

Relative Pronouns				
who	whose	which	that	whom
what	whoever	whatever	whichever	

Demonstrative pronouns point out particular persons or things, as in *that road* used in the literature passage. *This* and *that* are singular demonstrative pronouns and *these* and *those* are plural demonstrative pronouns.

Demonstrative Pronouns
this   that   these   those

Underline the pronouns in the following sentences. Indicate if they are interrogative, relative, demonstrative, or personal pronouns.
1) Who could have done this?
2) The man saw a donkey that was standing nearby.
3) What should be done next?
4) The innkeeper observed their approach.
5) The good Samaritan went on his way.

2.
e. 1) Who (interrogative), this (demonstrative)
   2) that (relative)
   3) What (interrogative)
   4) their (personal)
   5) his (personal)

3. Today, you will begin writing a biblical fiction story based on the account of the Good Samaritan. First read the full account in Luke 10:25-37. Write your story as if you were an eyewitness of the events Jesus told about. You will be writing in the first person so expect to use the pronouns *I, me, my*, and *our*. You may place yourself anywhere in the story - as the traveling man, the Samaritan, or even as another possible observer who isn't mentioned (the innkeeper's daughter). I even had a student once who wrote from the viewpoint of the donkey!

4. a. You may continue working on your story. If you have finished, read what you wrote and make any changes that seem good to you.

    b. To get another perspective, choose a different character and write his account of this story.

5. a. Read the second story you wrote and make any necessary changes.

    b. Optional: On a separate piece of paper, take the literature passage from dictation again.

    c. Take a spelling test of the words you misspelled this week.

    d. Choose skills from the *Review Activities* on the next page.

Review Activities

Choose skills your student needs to review.

1. *Personal, Interrogative, and Demonstrative Pronouns*
   Place the following pronouns under these headings: Personal, Interrogative, Demonstrative.

he			
her	you	those	mine
who	my	they	its
what	she	their	these
him	I	which	whose
this	it	whom	our
that	your	we	you

2. *Possessive Pronouns*
   Which of the personal pronouns you listed are possessive pronouns?

1.

Personal- he, her, him, you, my, she, I, you, they, their, we, mine, our, you, it, your, they, its

Interrogative- who, what, which, whom, whose

Demonstrative- this, that, those, these

2. her, my, your, their, mine, our

3. *1st, 2nd, 3rd Persons*
   a. In Matthew 18: 21-35, Jesus teaches about forgiveness. The parable begins "For this reason the kingdom of heaven may be compared to a certain king who wished to settle accounts with his slaves." Verses 24-27 read:

   And when he had begun to settle them, there was brought to him one who owed him ten thousand talents. But since he did not have the means to repay, his lord commanded him to be sold, along with his wife and children and all that he had, and repayment to be made. The slave therefore falling down, prostrated himself before him, saying, "Have patience with me, and I will repay you everything." And the lord of that slave felt compassion and released him and forgave him the debt.

   In what person are these verses written?

   b. Rewrite verses 24-27 in the first person, as if you were the slave being forgiven.

   c. Underline the pronouns in the following paragraph and circle the antecedents.

   A man had two sons. He came to the first and said, "Son, go work today in the vineyard." He answered and said, "I will, sir," but he did not go. He came to the second and said the same thing. But he answered and said "I will not," yet he afterward regretted it and went.

3.
a. third person

b.
And when he had begun to settle them, I, who owed him ten thousand talents, was brought to him. But since I did not have means to pay, my lord commanded I be sold, along with my wife and children and all that I had, and repayment to be made. I, therefore falling down, prostrated myself before him, saying, "Have patience with me, and I will repay you everything." And my lord felt compassion and released me and forgave me the debt.

c. He (a man)
   He (first son)
   I (first son)
   he (first son)
   He (a man)
   he (second son)
   I (second son)
   he (second son)

✎ **Teacher's Note:** As your student completes each lesson, choose skills from the *Review Activities* that he needs. The *Review Activities* follow each lesson.

Della finished her cry and attended to her cheeks with the powder rag. She stood by the window and looked out dully at a gray cat walking a gray fence in a gray backyard. Tomorrow would be Christmas Day, and she had only $1.87 with which to buy Jim a present. She had been saving every penny she could for months, with this result. Twenty dollars a week doesn't go far. Expenses had been greater than she had calculated. They always are. Only $1.87 to buy a present for Jim. Her Jim. Many a happy hour she had spent planning for something nice for him.

The Gift of the Magi by O. Henry

1. a. Write the literature passage from dictation. Correct any errors. Add any misspelled words to your *Personal Spelling List.*

   b. Take a spelling test of the next ten words from the *Commonly Misspelled Words List* and add any misspelled words to your *Personal Spelling List.* Study the list during the week.

   c. **Contractions** are two words joined together by an apostrophe ('). The **apostrophe** takes the place of the missing letter(s). Find the contraction used in the literature passage. What two words do they represent?
   Ex: mustn't - must not

1.
c. doesn't - does not

2. a. All sentences have two foundational parts: the complete subject and the complete predicate. The **complete subject** tells who or what the sentence is about. The **complete predicate** tells something about the subject. Look at just the first part of the third sentence of the literature passage:

   Tomorrow would be Christmas Day.

   Underline the complete subject once and the complete predicate twice.

2.
a. Tomorrow <u>would be</u>
   <u>Christmas Day.</u>

b. The complete predicate contains the most vital part of the sentence - the **verb**. The easiest kind of verb to recognize is the **action verb**, a verb that expresses physical or mental activity (run, sing, laugh, think). Find and circle the verbs used in the first two sentences.

c. Look at this sentence, and underline the subject once and the verb twice.

  Della was kind.

Della is not "doing" something, but rather she is "being" something. The verb *was* does not express action, but expresses a state of being. Not all verbs state an action.

Being Verbs
am   is   are   was
were   be   being   been

d. A verb in a sentence may consist of more than one word. A **verb phrase** is a verb consisting of two or more words, containing the main verb and one or more **helping** (or auxiliary) **verbs**. **Being verbs** may also be used as helping verbs. Sometimes a verb phrase is interrupted by another word, often *not* or *n't*. *Not* and *n't* are never a part of the verb.

Helping Verbs					
have	has	had	do	did	does
shall	will	could	would		
should	may	might	must	can	

In our literature passage, the sentence beginning "Tomorrow would be Christmas Day," *would be* is a verb phrase. Underline the other verb phrases in the literature passage.

2.
b. finished, attended, stood, looked

c. <u>Della</u> <u>was</u>

d. had been saving
   does (n't) go
   had been
   had calculated
   had spent

3. a & b.
Answer is found at the end of this lesson.

3. a. Verbs change their forms in order to show the time of an action. These forms of verbs are called **tenses**. Every verb has four principle parts: the **infinitive** (or base), the **present participle** (the **-ing** form used with a form of the verb *be*), the **past**, and the **past participle** (the **-ed** form used with a form of the verb *have*).

Complete this chart using verbs from the literature passage.

Infinitive	Present Participle	Past	Past Participle
Ex: finish	finishing	finished	(have) finished
attend			
look			
save			
calculate			
plan			

b. Verbs are classified as regular or irregular depending upon the way their past and past participle tenses are formed. The present participles are all formed the same way. The past and past participle tense of regular verbs are formed by adding **-ed** to their base form. The verbs you listed in **3a** are regular verbs.

An **irregular verb** is a verb that forms its past and past participle tense in some other way than a **regular verb**.

Complete this chart of irregular verbs.

Infinitive	Present Participle	Past	Past Participle
Ex: go	going	gone	(have) gone
stand			
think			
fly			
buy			
spend			

c. Everywhere Washington wears an air of expectancy. The hillocks of lumber, which have been piled for weeks along the Avenue, have finally been fashioned into grandstand and bleachers. Every street corner is garnished with the navy blue of District policemen. The gray lampposts are decorated with small American flags and pictures of Truman and Barkley. Red, white, and blue bunting are everywhere. In a few hours, forty thousand marchers and more than forty floats will form a column several miles long in honor of the President of the United States. It is Inauguration Day, January 20, 1949.

c. Look at the literature passage from Lesson 1. This is written in the past tense. The action has already taken place. Rewrite the paragraph in the present tense, as if the action is taking place right now.

4. a. Optional: Find a copy of the story, *The Gift of the Magi,* by
      O. Henry. This is easily accessible from your local library.
      It may be included in a collection of short stories written by
      the author. Read the story and then discuss it with your
      teacher.
      1) Would you say this was a happy story?
      2) Does this story teach any lessons or does it just
         entertain?
      3) If it teaches lessons, what are those lessons?
      4) How could the ending have been different?
      5) Did you like the story? Why or why not?

   b. If you are unfamiliar with the story, *The Gift of the Magi,*
      it is about a husband and wife who love each other
      dearly and want to purchase a nice Christmas gift for one
      another, but money is scarce. Try writing a paragraph of
      three or four sentences telling about Jim counting his
      money, thinking about what he can get for his wife,
      Della. The paragraph does not need to stay within the
      story line of *The Gift of the Magi.*

      Ex: Jim walked home from work. Despite the pain in his
          back, he thought about Della. He counted his money
          again, etc.

5. a. Using the verbs taken from the literature passage in
      Lesson 1, complete the chart. Indicate if they are regular
      (**R**) or irregular verbs (**IR**):

Infinitive	Present Participle	Past	Past Participle
Ex: serve R	serving	served	(have) served
Ex: find IR	finding	found	(have) found
wear			
fashion			
garnish			
decorate			
form			

   b. Optional: On a separate piece of paper, take the literature
      passage from dictation again.

   c. Take a spelling test of the words you misspelled this week.

4.
a. **Answers will vary. Allow
   for discussion.**

b. **Answers will vary.**

5.
a. **Answers are found at the
   end of this lesson.**

d. Points to Ponder

O. Henry was the pen name of William Sydney Porter, born in 1862. He published about 14 volumes of short stories known for sharp, unexpected endings. His life was as colorful as any tale he created. His early life included work in his uncle's drugstore at 15 and then two years on a Texas ranch. He later moved to Austin, Texas where he worked as a bank clerk. He was to be charged with stealing bank funds in 1896. Instead of facing the charges and a probable pardon, because his mistakes were the result of poor bookkeeping instead of criminal intent, he fled to Honduras. When he returned because of his wife's poor health, he was arrested and spent three years in prison. He wrote stories even while in prison and upon his release went to New York to be a newspaper columnist and a short-story writer.

e. Optional: Enjoy reading more O. Henry stories today.

f. Choose skills from the *Review Activities* on the next page.

Answers:

3. a.

Infinitive	Present Participle	Past	Past Participle
attend	attending	attended	(have) attended
look	looking	looked	(have) looked
save	saving	saved	(have) saved
calculate	calculating	calculated	(have) calculated
plan	planning	planned	(have) planned

3. b.

Infinitive	Present Participle	Past	Past Participle
stand	standing	stood	(have) stood
think	thinking	thought	(have) thought
fly	flying	flew	(have) flown
buy	buying	bought	(have) bought
spend	spending	spent	(have) spent

5. a.

Infinitive	Present Participle	Past	Past Participle
wear (IR)	wearing	wore	(have) worn
fashion (R)	fashioning	fashioned	(have) fashioned
garnish (R)	garnishing	garnished	(have) garnished
decorate (R)	decorating	decorated	(have) decorated
form (R)	forming	formed	(have) formed

Review Activities

Choose skills your student needs to review.

1. *Simple Subject*
Underline the simple subject of each sentence in this literature passage from *The Gift of the Magi*:

    Suddenly she whirled from the window and stood before the glass. Her eyes were shining brilliantly, but her face had lost its color within twenty seconds.

2. *Verbs*

  a. Make a list of action verbs found in the literature passage above.

  b. Using the verbs you listed above, write the principal parts under the correct heading.

Infinitive   Present Participle   Past   Past Participle

  c. Which of the verbs are irregular?

3. *Present Tense*
Rewrite the literature passage from exercise 1 into the present tense.

---

1. she
   eyes, face

2.
a. whirled, stood, were shining, had lost

b. Infinitive- whirl, stand, shine, lose

   Present Participle- whirling, standing, shining, losing

   Past- whirled, stood, shone, lost

   Past Participle- (have) whirled, (have) stood, (have) shone, (have) lost

c. stood, shining, lost

3. Suddenly she whirls from the window and stands before the glass. Her eyes shine brilliantly, but her face loses its color within twenty seconds.

✎ **Teacher's Note:** As your student completes each lesson, choose skills from the *Review Activities* that he needs. The *Review Activities* follow each lesson.

Sara started toward her. She looked as if she were going to box Lavinia's ears. Perhaps she was. Her trick of pretending things was the joy of her life. She never spoke of it to girls she was not fond of. Her new "pretend" about being a princess was very near to her heart, and she was shy and sensitive about it. She had meant it to be rather a secret, and here was Lavinia deriding it before nearly all the school. She felt the blood rush up into her face and tingle in her ears. She only just saved herself. If you were a princess, you did not fly into rages. Her hand dropped, and she stood quite still a moment. When she spoke it was in a quiet, steady voice; she held her head up, and everybody listened to her.

A Little Princess by Frances Hodgson Burnett

1. a. Write the literature passage from dictation. Compare with the model, and make corrections if necessary. Add any misspelled words to your *Personal Spelling List*.

   b. Take a spelling test of the next ten words from the *Commonly Misspelled Words List*. Add the words you miss to your *Personal Spelling List* and study them this week.

   c. Why do you think quotation marks (" ") were used around the word *pretend*?

   d. Nouns and pronouns can show possession. The possessive case of most singular nouns is formed by adding an apostrophe and **s** (**'s**) to the noun. Find the possessive noun in the literature passage. What possessive pronoun is used throughout the literature passage?

1.

c. *Pretend* is being used in a special sense, as a noun instead of the verb it usually is.

d. Lavinia's ears
    her

2. a. A **complete sentence** expresses a complete thought and is
        made up of two parts: a complete subject and a complete
        predicate. The complete subject tells who or what the
        sentence is about and contains at least one noun or pronoun.
        The complete predicate tells something about the subject and
        contains at least one verb. Look at the first sentence of the
        literature passage. Whom is the sentence about? What does
        the rest of the sentence tell us about Sara?

    b. The main noun or pronoun in the complete subject is called
        the **simple subject**. Since *Sara* is the only word in the
        complete subject, it is also the simple subject. Underline the
        action word in the complete predicate. This is called the
        simple predicate or **verb**. We will use the terms *subject* for
        the simple subject and *verb* for the simple predicate.

    c. Write the subject and verb of the first five sentences of the
        literature passage.

    d. The sentence, "She looked as if she were going to box
        Lavinia's ears," may appear to have two subjects and two
        verbs: *She looked* and *she were going*. You should have
        indicated *She* as the subject and *looked* as the verb of the
        sentence. *As if she were going to box Lavinia's ears*, is a
        group of words with a subject and a verb that cannot stand
        alone as a complete sentence. This is called a **dependent
        clause**. Look back at the literature passage in Lesson 1.
        Find the dependent clause in the second sentence.

3. a. Incomplete sentences do not contain either a subject or verb;
        or they can be dependent clauses that do not complete an
        idea. Remember, a dependent clause (or subordinate clause)
        is a group of words with a subject and verb that cannot
        stand alone. Authors sometimes intentionally use
        incomplete sentences for emphasis or effect. For example,
        in the literature passage in Lesson 3, O. Henry uses an
        incomplete sentence. Can you find it? Although effective,
        this technique should be used sparingly.

2
a. Sara
   started toward her

b. started

**c. Subject - Sara; Verb -
   started
   Subject - She; Verb -
   looked
   Subject - she; Verb -
   was
   Subject - trick; Verb -
   was
   Subject - She; Verb -
   spoke**

**d. which had been
   piled for weeks
   along the Avenue**

3. a. Her Jim.

3.
b. 1) CS
   2) **Possible answer: He bought a bundle of twigs.**
   3) CS
   4) **Possible answer: They built their houses.**
   5) CS
   6) **Possible answer: The first two houses fell down.**
   7) CS
   8) **Possible answer: The pigs just laughed at the wolf.**

c. **finished and attended stood and looked**

✏ **Teacher's Note: At this point, your student is learning only the coordinating conjunctions. Some grammar books do not include *yet* and *so* as coordinating conjunctions.**

d. **Her new "pretend" about being a princess was very near to her heart⊙and she was shy and sensitive about it.**

She had meant it to be rather a secret⊙and here was Lavinia deriding it before nearly all the school.

Her hand dropped⊙and she stood quite still a moment.

When she spoke it was in a quiet , steady voice; she held her head up⊙ and everybody listened to her.

b. Most often you will use an incomplete sentence unintentionally; so it is important to be able to identify them. Using the following groups of words, write **CS** if the words form a complete sentence. If the words do not form a complete sentence, add whatever it takes to complete the thought.
Ex: The day was sunny but cold.   **CS**
       Walked briskly down the hill. *The doctor walked briskly down the hill.*

1) The first pig bought a load of straw.
2) Bought a bundle of twigs.
3) The third pig purchased bricks.
4) Built their houses.
5) A hungry wolf came along.
6) The first two houses.
7) The brick house stood firm.
8) Just laughed at the wolf.

c. Complete sentences can have more than one subject and/or more than one verb. When a sentence has two subjects sharing one verb, it is said to have a **compound subject**. A sentence with two verbs having the same subject has a **compound verb**. Look at the first two sentences of the literature passage in Lesson 3. Find the compound verbs.

d. A **simple sentence** is a sentence which expresses one complete thought. Two or more simple sentences joined together is called a **compound sentence**. This is usually done with a connecting word called a **conjunction**.

Commonly Used Conjunctions						
and	but	or	nor	for	yet	so

In a compound sentence, a comma usually precedes the conjunction. If the word *and* can be omitted and the group of words following it can stand alone as a complete sentence, then *and* is being used to form a compound sentence. Highlight all the compound sentences. Circle the comma before the conjunction in each compound sentence of the literature passage.

e. Sometimes an author will choose a punctuation mark to join a compound sentence. Can you name the punctuation mark used to make the last sentence of the literature passage a compound sentence? A **semicolon** (;) may be used to connect two independent clauses without using a conjunction to form a compound sentence. An **independent clause** is one which can stand alone as a sentence.

4. a. Writing, like music, has a certain rhythm. The rhythm is controlled by the length of the sentences. Short sentences create a fast pace, while longer sentences slow the pace of the writing. Your writing will be more interesting if you vary the length of your sentences. Notice how Frances Hodgson Burnett varies the length of her sentences.

b. One way to vary the length of your sentences is by forming compound sentences. If this paragraph from *A Little Princess* did not contain any compound sentences, it would be rather boring. Rewrite the compound sentences you found yesterday in **3d** as simple sentences. Then read the passage inserting these simple sentences. You will hear how the "rhythm" of the paragraph changes.

c. Sentences are combined using conjunctions which include *and, or, but, for, nor*, and sometimes *yet* and *so*. Almost any two sentences can be combined by using the conjunction *and*. However, sentences combined in this way should be closely related. When they are not, you end up with **faulty coordination**. Another example of faulty coordination would be combining two simple sentences with an incorrect or weak conjunction.

Choose the best conjunction to make compound sentences. Write the new sentence.
1) I was hungry. The refrigerator was empty.
2) The day was cold. I put on a jacket.
3) Will the pitcher throw the ball to home? Will he throw it to first?
4) I play the piano. My sister plays the violin.

3.
e. semicolon

4.
b. Sara started toward her. She looked as if she were going to box Lavinia's ears. Perhaps she was. Her trick of pretending things was the joy of her life. She never spoke of it to girls she was not fond of. Her new "pretend" about being a princess was very near to her heart. She was shy and sensitive about it. She had meant it to be rather a secret. Here was Lavinia deriding it before nearly all the school. She felt the blood rush up into her face and tingle in her ears. She only just saved herself. If you were a princess, you did not fly into rages. Her hand dropped. She stood quite still a moment. When she spoke it was in a quiet, steady voice. She held her head up. Everybody listened to her.

c. 1) I was hungry, but the refrigerator was empty.
2) The day was cold, so I put on a jacket.
3) Will the pitcher throw the ball to home, or will he throw it to first?
4) I play the piano, and my sister plays the violin.

4.

d. Possible answer: Sara
started toward her and
she looked as if she were
going to box Lavinia's
ears. Perhaps she was,
for her trick of pretending
things was the joy of her
life; and she never spoke
of it to girls she was not
fond of. Her new
"pretend" about being a
princess was very near to
her heart and she was shy
and sensitive about it.
She had meant it to be
rather a secret and here
was Lavinia deriding it
before nearly all the
school. She felt the
blood rush up into her
face and tingle in her
ears. She only just saved
herself. If you were a
princess, you did not fly
into rages, so her hand
dropped. She stood quite
still a moment, and when
she spoke it was in a
quiet steady voice. She
held her head up, and
everybody listened to her.

The meaning does not
change.
Allow for discussion.

e. *tingle in her ears* cannot
stand alone

d. Almost all the simple sentences in the literature passage could be joined with *and*. Try rewriting the literature passage by making the simple sentences into compound sentences and changing some of the compound sentences into simple sentences. Does this change the meaning of the paragraph? What does it do to the "rhythm" of the paragraph? Which do you like better?

e. Look at this sentence taken from the literature passage:

She felt the blood rush up into her face and tingle in her ears.

This sentence contains the conjunction *and*, but it is not a compound sentence. Why?

5. a. Using context clues, explain what "here was Lavinia deriding it before nearly all the school" means.

   b. This story is written in the third person, as if an outside viewer were telling it. Rewrite the story in the first person, as if you were Sara telling what happened.

   c. Optional: On a separate piece of paper, take the literature passage from dictation again.

   d. Take a spelling test using the words you misspelled this week.

   e. Choose skills from the *Review Activities* on the next page.

5.

a. Sara was very sensitive about her make believe game and didn't want just anyone to know about it. She knew not everyone would understand. When Lavinia found out about it, she made fun of it in front of all of Sara's classmates.

b. I started toward her. I looked as if I were going to box Lavinia's ears. Perhaps I was. My trick of pretending things was the joy of my life. I never spoke of it to girls I was not fond of. My new "pretend" about being a princess was very near to my heart, and I was shy and sensitive about it. I had meant it to be rather a secret, and here was Lavinia deriding it before nearly all the school. I felt the blood rush up into my face and tingle in my ears. I only just saved myself. If you were a princess, you did not fly into rages. My hand dropped, and I stood quite still a moment. When I spoke it was in a quiet, steady voice; I held my head up, and everybody listened to me.

Review Activities

Choose skills your student needs to review.

1. *Possessive Noun and Possessive Pronoun*
   Write the possessive noun or pronoun for the following:

   a. the tools that belong to Jim
   b. the car that belongs to him
   c. the shoes that belong to Sally
   d. the wings that belong to the bees
   e. the room that belongs to David and Jesse
   f. the house that belongs to that family
   g. the books that belong to my sister and me
   h. the dog that belongs to you

2. *Conjunctions*
   Circle the conjunctions in the following sentences
   taken from *A Little Princess*:

   a. She went back to her seat and opened the book.
   b. She sat down upon the floor and turned the key.
   c. Refreshments were not likely to be disdained at any hour and many pairs of eyes gleamed.
   d. Several of the other children began to cry, but she did not seem to hear them or to be alive to anything.
   e. The change in her life did not come about gradually but was made all at once.

3. *Compound Sentence*
   Which of the sentences above is a compound sentence?

1.

   a. Jim's tools
   b. his car
   c. Sally's shoes
   d. bees' wings
   e. David and Jesse's room
   f. family's house
   g. our books
   h. your dog

2.

   a. and
   b. and
   c. and
   d. but, or
   e. but

3. Sentence d is a compound sentence.

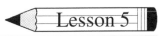

They climbed on in silence for a time. Soon they would reach the lower plain, and then Onesimus would look up and see the outskirts of Colosse and the canyons and the meadows, bright with marigolds and daisies, where Philemon's sheep grazed. Already he could hear the crying of half-grown lambs, the bleating of the dams, and the rushing of the stream where he had loved to play as a little boy. How he had sometimes longed for these sights and sounds in Rome! Now, they only filled him with dread and foreboding.

Twice Freed by Patricia St. John
(Used by permission, Moody Press)

1. a. Take this literature passage from dictation. Compare with the model and correct. Add any misspelled words to your *Personal Spelling List*.

   b. Take a spelling test of the next ten words from the *Commonly Misspelled Words List*. Add any misspelled words to your *Personal Spelling List*.

   c. Vocabulary Builder - foreboding

   Using the context clues and your own knowledge, write a dictionary sounding definition for the word *foreboding*. You may look up the *Word Parts List* in the *Appendix* for extra clues. Now look up the word in the *Glossary*. Write a sentence using the word.

2. a. Look at the first sentence of the literature passage. Underline the subject once and the verb twice. This sentence is an independent clause. That means it expresses a complete thought and can stand on its own (independent). It is a simple sentence, expressing one complete thought.

   b. The second sentence is not a simple sentence. Why? There are two independent clauses joined by the conjunction *and*. This is a compund sentence. Underline the subject once and the verb twice in each clause. The second clause contains two verbs.

Teacher's Note: As your student completes each lesson, choose skills from the *Review Activities* that he needs. The *Review Activities* follow each lesson.

1.
c. *foreboding* - foretelling: usually something bad

2.
a. They climbed

b. they would reach

   Onesimus would look and see

c. Like independent clauses, dependent clauses contain a subject and verb; but unlike independent clauses, they cannot stand alone. They do not express a complete thought.

Look at this sentence taken from the literature passage:

> *Already he could hear the crying of half-grown lambs, the bleating of dams, and the rushing of the stream where he had loved to play as a little boy.*

Draw parentheses around the dependent clause. Underline the subject once and the verb twice.

2.

c. (where he had loved to play as a little boy)

d. he could hear

e. (where Philemon's sheep grazed)

d. The remainder of the sentence, "Already he could hear the crying of half-grown lambs ... stream" is an independent clause. Underline the subject once and the verb twice.

e. There is another dependent clause in the literature passage. Draw parentheses around it.

f. Dependent clauses can be used in several different ways in a sentence. They can act as adjectives, adverbs, or nouns. An **adjective clause** modifies or describes a noun or pronoun, usually introduced by a relative pronoun.
   Ex: Onesimus, *who had been a runaway slave*, knew what it was to be forgiven.

Relative Pronouns				
who	whose	which	what	that
whoever	whatever	whichever		

An **adverb clause** modifies or describes a verb, adjective, or another adverb. It usually tells how, when, where, why, or to what extent an action takes place.
   Ex: *After meeting Paul*, Onesimus was ready to return to Philemon.

Noun clauses function as nouns in a sentence. These clauses usually cannot be removed from the sentence without making it meaningless.
   Ex: *Asking for forgiveness* is not always an easy thing to do.

g. You found a dependent clause in **2c** and **2e**. What kind of clauses are they?

2.
g. Both are adverb
   clauses

3. a. Read the letter Paul wrote to Philemon in the New Testament. (This is the book of Philemon.) This is a personal letter containing greetings, news, and special requests. Although we live in an electronic age with telephones and e-mail, there are times when it is necessary to write a letter. There are two basic types of letters: the friendly letter and the business letter.

   b. **Friendly letters** are personal and may serve several different purposes, such as to convey news, answer questions, issue an invitation, or to say thank you. These letters do not necessarily follow a formal standard. The following elements make up most friendly letters.

      1) **Heading** - This is your address and is written on two lines in the upper right-hand corner. The city and state are separated by a comma. The zip code follows. Do not put a comma between the state and the zip code. On the third line, write the date with a comma between the day of the month and the year. No other punctuation is needed.

      2) **Greeting or Salutation** - This is the greeting, usually begun with *Dear* _____. The greeting is flush with the left-hand margin a few lines below the heading. Put a comma after the salutation.

      3) **Body** - The first line of the body of the letter should be indented, as should the first line of each succeeding paragraph. All other lines begin at the left-hand margin.

      4) **Closing** - Place the closing a few lines below the body, lined up underneath the heading. Capitalize the first word of the closing and put a comma at the end. Common closings include *Sincerely, Your friend, Love*, or something similar.

      5) **Signature** - Sign your name beneath the closing. Do not put any punctuation after your name.

✎ Teacher's Note: Today, the two-letter postal abbreviation for states is more commonly used than the three-letter abbreviation. Either is acceptable, but advise your student to use them carefully.
Ex: Florida - Fla. - Begins with a capital letter and ends with a period.
FL - Both letters are in capital letters and does *not* end with a period.

c. Label the parts of this friendly letter using the corresponding numbers for the parts of a letter:

1) heading   2) greeting   3) body   4) closing   5) signature

3.
c. 1) Heading
   2) Salutation or greeting
   3) Body
   4) Closing
   5) Signature

Hundred Acre Wood
Imagi, Nation   11111 ____
April 1, 1997

Dear Pooh Bear, ____

   To celebrate your getting thin again, I have planned a Grand Celebration. Can you come? I have invited Rabbit and all of his friends and relations, along with Owl and Tigger. Of course, you may bring Dear Piglet with you, Silly Old Bear. ____

                                   My regards, ____
                                   Christopher Robin ____

---

d. Think of a friend or family member to whom you would like to write. On a separate piece of paper, write a short letter to him. Remember to include all the elements of a friendly letter.

4. a. The second type of letter is the business letter. **Business letters** should always be clear, concise, and courteous. There are many styles of business letters, but you will learn the widely used Block Style.

The following elements make up a business letter:

1) **Heading** - This is the same as a friendly letter but is written on the left-hand margin.

2) **Inside Address** - Unlike a friendly letter, business letters have an inside address of the person or business to whom you are writing. This is placed a short space below the heading and flush with the left-hand margin.

3) **Greeting or Salutation** - The salutation is placed two spaces below the inside address, flush with the left-hand margin. It is followed with a colon (**:**). If you are writing to a business rather than an individual, you may use an impersonal salutation (Ex. *Shipping* or *Gentlemen*). If you do not know the name of the person you are writing to, the salutation may be *Dear Sir* or *Dear Madam.*

4) **Body** - Each paragraph begins flush on the left-hand margin. Indicate a new paragraph by double spacing.

5) **Closing** - The usual closing of a business letter is *Yours truly* or *Very truly yours.* Only the first word is capitalized. The closing is placed two lines below the body, flush on the left-hand margin. It should be followed by a comma.

6) **Signature** - If you have typed the letter, type your name about four lines below the closing, leaving space to sign your name in ink between the closing and the typed signature. Do not use a title (Mr., Mrs., etc.) before your handwritten signature.

b. Label the parts of the following business letter:

4.
b. 1) Heading
   2) Inside Address
   3) Greeting or Salutation
   4) Body
   5) Closing
   6) Signature

County Court House
Pigville, PA 10001   _____
April 1, 1997

Uneeda Lawyer Agency
100 Easy Street   _____
Fair Judgment, PA 10022

Dear Sir: _____

Your agency has come highly recommended to me. I
am writing to ask you to please take my case. I have
been accused of destroying property, namely two
houses. I assure you, I am innocent. I was framed by
a pig living in a brick house. Can you assist me?
You may reach me at the above address.

Thank you for your consideration. _____

Sincerely, _____

B.B. Wolf

_____

B. B. Wolf

c. On a separate piece of paper, write a letter to your state's
   Chamber of Commerce requesting information about the
   historical and recreational opportunities in the state. Your
   letter should be addressed to:

      Chamber of Commerce
      State of _____
      Capital City, State Zip

d. The envelope for a friendly or business letter should be addressed in the same form. You should take great care to be neat and clear. Place the address of the person to whom you are writing just below the middle and to the left of the center of the envelope. Place your own name and address in the upper left-hand corner. No title is used before your name.

B.B. Wolf   STAMP
County Court House
Pigville, PA 10001

                          Uneeda Lawyer Agency
                          100 Easy Street
                          Fair Judgment, PA 10022

---

5. a. Optional: On a separate piece of paper, take the literature passage from dictation again.

   b. Take a spelling test of the words you misspelled this week.

   c. On a separate piece of paper, write a thank you letter for a gift or favor you have recently received. Address it, stamp it, and with your teacher's permission, mail it.

   d. Copy the following paragraph from *Twice Freed*. Underline the subjects once and verbs twice. Draw parentheses around the dependent clauses.

      They paused for a hasty meal outside the city, but not for long, for the weather was getting more and more strange. The sky was a smoky red, like some weird, lost sunset, although it was only shortly after midday. The streets were almost empty, for the air in the city was oppressive and most people were indoors taking a siesta. Glaucus, panting and perspiring and glancing at the sky, was very unhappy indeed.

   e. Choose skills from the *Review Activities* on the next page.

5.
d. They <u>paused</u> for a hasty meal outside the city, (but not for long,) for the <u>weather</u> <u>was</u> <u>getting</u> more and more strange. The <u>sky</u> <u>was</u> a smoky red, like some weird, lost sunset, although <u>it</u> <u>was</u> only shortly after midday. The <u>streets</u> <u>were</u> almost empty, for the <u>air</u> in the city <u>was</u> oppressive and most <u>people</u> <u>were</u> indoors taking a siesta. <u>Glaucus</u>, (panting and perspiring and glancing at the sky,) <u>was</u> very unhappy indeed.

Review Activities

Choose skills your student needs to review.

1. heading, greeting or salutation, body, closing, signature

1. *Friendly Letter*
   What are the five parts of a friendly letter?

2. heading, inside address, greeting or salutation, body, closing, signature

2. *Business Letter*
   What are the six parts of a business letter?

3. (It was good to have her home)

   (she told him as much as she could about the morning they had spent with Paul)

3. *Independent Clause*
   There are two independent clauses in this sentence from *Twice Freed*. Draw parentheses around them.

   It was good to have her home, and she told him as much as she could about the morning they had spent with Paul.

A broad ray of light fell into the garret, and showed the workman with an unfinished shoe upon his lap, pausing in his labor. His few common tools and various scraps of leather were at his feet and on his bench. He had a white beard, raggedly cut, but not very long, a hollow face, and exceedingly bright eyes. The hollowness and thinness of his face would have caused them to look large, under his yet dark eyebrows, and his confused white hair, though they had been really otherwise; but, they were naturally large, and looked unnaturally so. His yellow rags of shirt lay open at the throat, and showed his body to be withered and worn.

A Tale of Two Cities by Charles Dickens

1. a. Write the literature passage from dictation. Compare with the model, and make any necessary corrections. If you misspelled any words, add them to your *Personal Spelling List*.

   b. Take a spelling test of the next ten words from the *Commonly Misspelled Words List*. Add any words you miss to your *Personal Spelling List* and study them this week.

   c. Vocabulary Builder - garret, exceedingly

   Write a dictionary sounding definition for the words *garret* and *exceedingly* using the context clues and your own knowledge. Remember, you may be able to find more clues by checking the *Word Parts Lists* in the *Appendix*. When you are through, look up these words in the *Glossary*, and write a sentence using each word correctly.

Teacher's Note: As your student completes each lesson, choose skills from the *Review Activities* that he needs. The *Review Activities* follow each lesson.

1.
c. *garret* - that part of a house which is on the upper floor, immediately under the roof

   exceedingly - greatly

2. a. In grammar, words that modify limit or make nouns and
       pronouns more specific.

       modify - (L. *modus* - limit) to qualify, to reduce in extent

       Notice the difference in these three sentences:

            The apple lay in the bowl.
            The withered apple lay in the cracked bowl.
            The luscious apple lay in the silver bowl.

       Each sentence suggests a different picture. The first is rather
       vague. The next two are more specific. What words tell
       you what kind of apple? What words tell you what kind of
       bowl? These words are modifiers called **adjectives**.
       Adjectives answer the questions *what kind, how many, how
       much, which one*, or *whose*.

2.
a. *withered, luscious* apple

   cracked, silver bowl

   b. Find the answers to these questions in the literature passage.
       1) What kind of ray?
       2) What kind of shoe?
       3) What kind of tools?
       4) What kind of scraps?
       5) What kind of beard?
       6) What kind of face?
       7) What kind of eyes?
       8) What kind of eyebrows?
       9) What kind of hair?
      10) What kind of rags?

b. 1) *broad* ray
2) *unfinished* shoe
3) *few, common* tools
4) *various* scraps
5) *white* beard
6) *hollow* face (*thin*)
7) *bright* eyes
8) *dark* eyebrows
9) *confused white* hair
10) *yellow* rags

   c. The most commonly used adjectives are *a, an,* and *the*.
       These special adjectives are called **articles**. Almost every
       sentence contains at least one article. Notice how *a* and *an*
       are used in the literature passage. When do you use *an*
       instead of *a*?

c. Use *an* before a word
   that begins with a vowel
   or vowel sound.
   Otherwise, use *a*.
   Ex: an apple; an honor;
   a chair

   d. In Lesson 2, you studied possessive pronouns. Possessive
       pronouns modify nouns answering the question *whose*.

       Circle the possessive pronoun in the literature passage.

d. his

e. The last question which modifiers answer is *how much*. Circle the adjective in the second sentence of the literature passage that tells you how many tools the workman had.

2.
e. few

f. Choose a person in the room, or look in a mirror, and describe what you see. Write three sentences describing what you see.
   Ex: A warm face greets me with a friendly smile. Long, dark curls frame a healthy, dark complexion.

3. a. As you learned yesterday, adjectives give us important information. They make your writing more vivid and interesting. Today you will spend time working with adjectives in preparation for tomorrow's assignment.

   Write three adjectives describing these nouns.
   Ex: *decrepit, palatial, haunted*   house
   1) _____ noise
   2) _____ animals
   3) _____ queen
   4) _____ street

3. a. Possible answers:
   1) loud, irritating, suspicious
   2) several, tame, ferocious
   3) victorious, humble, elegant
   4) quiet, dark, unfamiliar

b. In order to do these exercises, you will need a thesaurus. Anyone who wishes to improve his writing should have access to a good dictionary and a thesaurus. It has been said that a dictionary provides the meanings of words, while a thesaurus provides words for given meanings. The word *thesaurus* is from Latin meaning "a storehouse of knowledge." It will help you choose just the right word. Using a thesaurus regularly will help improve your vocabulary.

   Using your thesaurus, find adjectives that are more specific than the ones given.
   Ex: (bad) *dreadful, inadequate, terrible*   singer
   1) (pretty) _____ dress
   2) (sad) _____ story
   3) (dear) _____ child
   4) (lowly) _____ cottage

b. Possible answers:
1) attractive, lovely, beautiful
2) poignant, woeful, moving
3) beloved, cherished, precious
4) humble, unpretentious, modest

3.

c. Possible answers:

1) unattractive, grotesque, ugly
2) happy, uplifting, cheerful
3) despised, vile, hateful
4) opulent, palatial, affluent

d. Suggestions:

nice - admirable, likable, delightful, fine

good - commendable, virtuous, exemplary, favorable

c. Antonyms are words of opposite meaning. A thesaurus also lists any possible antonyms. Using your thesaurus, write three antonyms for the adjectives in **3b**.
    Ex: (bad) *wholesome, satisfactory, excellent* singer

d. Two of the most overused adjectives are *nice* and *good*. Look up these words in your thesaurus and make a list of synonyms for each one. In future writing assignments, try to use these new words in place of *nice* and *good*.

e. Finally, as useful as adjectives are, you can get carried away and use too many. Instead of making your writing more clear, your writing becomes so cumbersome it will be distracting.
    Ex: The slender, attractive, golden-haired woman took a big, noisy, juicy bite out of the shiny, red, delicious looking apple that was lying on the ornate, silver platter.

Remember, choose your words carefully!

f. Using the words you found in the thesaurus in **3b**, write a few sentences.

4. a. Today you will write a description of someone you know well. You can describe the person in a specific place or doing some task. The **character sketch** should go beyond the way the person looks and create an emotional response in your reader.

   Ex: Johnny slumped in his chair. His disheveled hair looked as if it hadn't been combed in weeks. He placed his elbow on the desk and rested his chin on the palm of his hand. His yawn revealed a much needed visit to the dentist.

   b. After you have finished writing your description, read it over. Note the adjectives you used. Are they specific? You may want to use your thesaurus to "sharpen" the picture you have painted.

5. a. Take a spelling test of the words you misspelled this week.

   b. Turn to the literature passage in Lesson 2. Make a list of adjectives that might describe the following people in this story:
      1) the man before he was attacked
      2) the man after he was attacked
      3) the robbers
      4) the Priest and/or Levite
      5) the Samaritan

   c. Optional: On a separate piece of paper, take the literature passage from dictation again.

   d. Choose skills from the *Review Activities* on the next page.

5.
b. 1) wealthy, solitary, apprehensive, etc.
   2) broken, lonely, destitute, etc.
   3) sly, greedy, cruel, etc.
   4) selfish, unconcerned, fastidious, etc.
   5) unselfish, kind, benevolent, etc.

Review Activities

Choose skills your student needs to review.

1. articles
   the, a, an

1. *Adjectives*
    Fill in the blanks: The most commonly used adjectives are
    called _____. These are ____, _____, and
    _____.

2. and 3.
   sumptuous (what kind)
   Thirty (how many)
   his (whose)
   twenty-four (how many)
   male (what kind)
   his (whose)
   six (how many)
   his (whose)
   his (whose)
   matrimonial (what kind)
   social (what kind)
   greatest (how much)
   that (which one)

2. Underline the adjectives in this paragraph from *A Tale of Two Cities*. (Ignore the articles.)

    A sumptuous man was the Farmer-General. Thirty horses stood in his stables, twenty-four male domestics sat in his halls, six body-women waited on his wife. As one who pretended to do nothing but plunder and forage where he could, the Farmer-General — howsoever his matrimonial relations conduced to social morality — was at least the greatest reality among the personages who attended at the hotel of Monseigneur that day.

3. What question does each adjective answer?

Oh say, can you see by the dawn's early light,
What so proudly we hailed at the twilight's last gleaming?
Whose broad stripes and bright stars thru the perilous fight
O'er the ramparts we watched, were so gallantly streaming?
And the rocket's red glare, the bombs bursting in air,
Gave proof thru the night that our flag was still there,
Oh say, does that star-spangled banner yet wave,
O'er the land of the free and the home of the brave?

"Star-Spangled Banner" by Francis Scott Key

1. a. Write this familiar song from dictation. Compare to the model and make any necessary corrections. Add any misspelled words to your *Personal Spelling List*.

   b. This week will be a Spelling Review week. Take a test of all the words from the *Commonly Misspelled Words List* which you missed to this point. Add the ones you miss to your *Personal Spelling List* and study them during the week.

   c. Practice singing the song.

2. a. Vocabulary Builder - perilous, ramparts

   Write a dictionary sounding definition for each word using the context clues and your own knowledge. Now look up the word in the *Glossary*. Write a sentence using each word.

   b. Use your encyclopedia or history book to find out the following information. Write down your answers to each question. You should be able to find the information by looking up the title and the author of the piece.
   1) Who wrote the words of "The Star-Spangled Banner?"
   2) When were they written?
   3) Who set it to this music?
   4) When was it adopted as our national anthem?
   5) Under what conditions were the words written?

2
a. *perilous* - dangerous
   ramparts - embankment

b. 1) The "Star-Spangled Banner" was written by Francis Scott Key, a lawyer.
   2) It was written during the War of 1812.
   3) The music was written by John Stafford Smith.
   4) Congress officially approved the song as the national anthem in March, 1931.
   5) Key had boarded a prisoner-exchange boat to plead for the release of a friend who had been captured by the British. The boat was held in temporary custody in Baltimore Harbor, so Key was able to witness the British bombardment of Fort McHenry from this vantage point. In 1814, after a night of shelling, Key was overjoyed to find the American flag still flying and was inspired to pen these words. The words were distributed on handbills soon after completion. Shortly after, it was set to music.

c. Using the information you gathered, write a paragraph about the history of "The Star-Spangled Banner." Begin your paragraph by introducing the **topic**. This is called the **topic sentence**. All the other sentences should support the topic sentence. These are called **supporting sentences**. Don't forget to **indent** the first sentence of your paragraph.

3. a. In your own words, write what you think the author is saying in this verse of "The Star-Spangled Banner."

b. Work on memorizing the verse until you can write it or sing it from memory.

4. a. Because "The Star-Spangled Banner" is difficult to sing, it has been suggested we choose another song as our national anthem, such as "God Bless America," or "America the Beautiful." Do you agree? Why or why not?

b. Today you will write a **persuasive paper** expressing your thoughts. What you are trying to do is to get others to see things the way you do.

A persuasive paper can take three different approaches:
1) an appeal to emotion
2) an appeal to reason
3) an appeal by authority

These three approaches will overlap. For example, an emotional appeal will require evidence to support your position. Conversely, a reasoned appeal will not lack emotion. An emotional appeal could include words about patriotism and nostalgia. A reasoned appeal should be based on facts, such as the ease of understanding the words or singing the song. An appeal to authority might mention our forefathers and quote what they had to say.

c. On a separate piece of paper, begin writing a first draft stating your views about why we should keep "The Star-Spangled Banner" as our national anthem or why it would be a good idea to choose another song. After writing your paper, put it aside for revising tomorrow.

3.

a. Sample answer: This is the cry of the poet's heart. His last good look at the flag was just at twilight. Since that time the fort had been shelled continuously. As the exploding bombs gave a flash of light, he was able to see that the flag was still proudly flying. The morning is coming, is the flag still waving indicating victory for the Americans?

4.

a. Allow time for discussion.

5. a. Take a spelling test of the words you misspelled this week.

b. It is always a good idea to put your work aside for a time before attempting to revise it. You will have a fresh feel for it after distancing yourself from it. Read your paper. Ask yourself these questions:
   1) What are my main points?
   2) Are they clearly expressed?
   3) Do my arguments support my main points?

c. Now have someone else read your paper and discuss any changes he suggests.

Teacher's Note: Review Activities for Lesson 7 aren't necessary.

d. Next, check your paper for any spelling, capitalization, and punctuation errors. Write your final draft.

Assessment 1
(Lessons 1-7)

1. Write five common nouns.

2. Write five proper nouns.

3. Rewrite the following paragraph from *A Man Called Peter,* and add the correct capitalization and punctuation:

   the railway express truck rumbled up pleasant road and stopped before an obviously new cape cod cottage. it was a gray-shingled house with green blinds nestling atop a gently rising slope. the driver of the truck climbed out and began unloading a number of heavy cartons. mr. robert ingraham who had a summer home just up the road stood watching with undisguised interest.

4. Write a sentence with an introductory phrase.

5. Place these pronouns under the appropriate heading:

   I   he   you   them   him   she   her   it   us

First Person	Second Person	Third Person

6. Write a sentence with an interrogative pronoun.

7. Replace the italicized words with pronouns:
   a. Faith thought the present was for *Faith.*
   b. After reading the book, Eddie put *the book* back on the shelf.
   c. Ruth skinned *Ruth's* knee when *Ruth* fell.
   d. When Will saw Sara, *Will* gave *Sara* a big hug.
   e. Bob and Jill painted *Bob and Jill's* house.

Answers (left column):

1. Possible answers: shoe, car, book, city, girl

2. Possible answers: Keds, Caravan, Bible, Paris, Jill

3. The Railway Express truck rumbled up Pleasant Road and stopped before an obviously new Cape Cod cottage. It was a gray-shingled house with green blinds, nestling atop a gently rising slope. The driver of the truck climbed out and began unloading a number of heavy cartons. Mr. Robert Ingraham, who had a summer home just up the road, stood watching with undisguised interest.

4. Possible answer: Upon receiving the good news, Pat decided a celebration was in order.

5. *First Person* - I, us, *Second Person* - you *Third Person* - he, him, them, she, her, it

6. Possible answers: *Who* goes there? *Whose* car is this? *Which* of the books did you like best? *What* are you doing?

7. a. Faith thought the present was for *her.*
   b. After reading the book, Eddie put *it* back on the shelf.
   c. Ruth skinned *her* knee when *she* fell.
   d. When Will saw Sara, *he* gave *her* a big hug.
   e. Bob and Jill painted *their* house.

8. Make a list of action verbs found in the following literature passage taken from *Twice Freed*:

> Philemon glanced at the prostrate goldsmith with extreme distaste and then turned to the white-faced boy in fetters and gazed at him thoughtfully. Onesimus had grown up with his own son and had tumbled around his footstool in babyhood. He was surprised at his own reluctance to sentence this slave.

9. Using the verbs you listed in exercise 8, write the principal parts under the correct heading. Indicate if the verbs are regular (**R**) or irregular (**IR**):

Infinitive	**Present Participle**	**Past**	**Past Participle**
Ex: glance (**R**)	glancing	glanced	(have) glanced

10. Underline the subject of each sentence in the literature passage used in exercise 8 above.

11. Which of the following are complete sentences?
    a. Getting up early.
    b. Mark planned to go to the beach.
    c. He drove to his favorite spot.
    d. Before the crowds came.
    e. He swam and sunned for two hours.
    f. Then the sky grew dark.
    g. Running to his car.
    h. He jumped in.
    i. Just as the first raindrop fell.

12. a. Join a dependent and independent clause from exercise 11, and make two or three sentences.

    b. Underline the dependent clauses in exercise 11, and indicate if they are adverb or adjective clauses.

8. and 9.
Answers are found at the end of this lesson.

10. Philemon, Onesimus, He

11. b, c, e, f, h

12.
a. Possible answers: Getting up early, Mark planned to go to the beach. He drove to his favorite spot before the crowds came. Running to his car, he jumped in just as the first raindrop fell.

b. getting up early (adjective)
before the crowds came (adverb)
Running to his car (adjective)
just as the first raindrop fell (adverb)

13. the address of the person sending the letter and the date the letter was written

14. Possible answer: Dear Sir:

15. Possible answer: Yours truly,

16. what kind, how many, how much, which one, whose

17. <u>his</u> (head)
<u>his</u>, <u>courtly</u> (manner)
<u>his</u>, <u>smiling</u> (face)
<u>those</u> (words)
<u>his</u> (nephew)
<u>same</u> (time)
<u>thin</u>, <u>straight</u> (lines)
<u>thin</u>, <u>straight</u> (lips)

✏ Teacher's Note: The word *smiling* in this text is a verb form used as an adjective. This is called a participle and will be discussed in Lesson 21.

18. He bends his head in his most courtly manner, there is a secrecy in his smiling face, and he conveys an air of mystery to those words, which strikes the eyes and ears of his nephew forcibly. At the same time, the thin straight lines of the setting of the eyes, and the thin straight lips, and the markings in the nose, curve with a sarcasm that looks handsomely diabolic.

13. What information does the heading in a letter contain?

14. Write an example of a salutation in a business letter.

15. Write an example of a closing in a business letter.

16. What questions do adjectives answer?

17. Underline the adjectives in this literature passage from *A Tale of Two Cities*. (Do not include articles.) What nouns do they modify?

As he bent his head in his most courtly manner, there was a secrecy in his smiling face, and he conveyed an air of mystery to those words, which struck the eyes and ears of his nephew forcibly. At the same time, the thin straight lines of the setting of the eyes, and the thin straight lips, and the markings of the nose, curved with a sarcasm that looked handsomely diabolic.

18. Rewrite the literature passage in the present tense.

Answer 8. and 9.

Infinitive	Present Participle	Past	Past Participle
glance (R)	glancing	glanced	(have) glanced
turn (R)	turning	turned	(have) turned
gaze (R)	gazing	gazed	(have) gazed
grow (IR)	growing	grew	(have) grown
tumble (R)	tumbling	tumbled	(have) tumbled
suprise (R)	suprising	suprised	(have) suprised

BOOK STUDY

on

Across Five Aprils

Across Five Aprils
By Irene Hunt
Published by Follett
Publishing Co.

We suggest that you keep a map of the United States available as you read the book. You may follow the major events of the Civil War by finding the places mentioned in the story.

Summary

It was April of 1861. Nine-year-old Jethro Creighton, working with his mother in the field, thought the world a fine place. The youngest child in a large, loving family, he enjoyed working on the family's farm in southern Illinois. He also enjoyed attending the small school nearby which was taught by his hero, Shadrach Yale, who saw great potential in the young boy. But all was not fine in the world that April of 1861. There was talk of war and what it would mean, not only to the country, but to the Creighton family and their neighbors as well.

After the firing upon Fort Sumter in South Carolina, Jethro's older brothers begin to leave the farm to enlist, all but one joining the Northern army. Jethro's favorite brother, Bill, struggling with the issues, decides that he must join the Rebel cause. Bill's leaving causes much grief to his family as well as bringing persecution from men who feel the family should disown Bill. As the Aprils go by, Jethro grows quickly from a little boy to a young man, learning to face the many fears the war brings, grief at the loss of a brother, and the responsibility of managing the farm when his father experiences a heart attack and can no longer work.

Mrs. Hunt tells a moving story of childhood lost and the price that was paid by all during the saddest period of our country's history. She relates that the background of *Across Five Aprils* came from letters and records she found, as well as from the stories told by her own grandfather who was, like Jethro, a boy of nine when the war began. As you read *Across Five Aprils*, you will gain a clear understanding of the conflict known as the Civil War.

Vocabulary

Find the word in its context. Reread the sentences before and after the word. What do you think the word means? Look up the word in the dictionary and write a clear, simple definition, and use it in a sentence.

1. seceding - (pg. 14)

2. pompous - (pg. 61)

3. genially - (pg. 123)

4. interminable - (pg. 144)

5. tenacity - (pg. 176)

Complete the sentences with the correct vocabulary word. OR Write your own sentences using the vocabulary words.

6. The students shifted in their seats as they waited for the professor to end his _____ lecture.

7. The gentleman's _____ behavior made the young men feel insignificant.

8. Father smiled and greeted the stranger _____.

9. Life appeared unstable as the states were _____ from the Union.

10. The young boy's _____ was not tolerated by his baby-sitter.

1. **withdrawing from the Union**

2. **appearing pretentious and grand**

3. **cheerfully**

4. **boringly long**

5. **persistence of being stubborn**

6. **interminable**
7. **pompous**
8. **genially**
9. **seceding**
10. **tenacity**

1. Some events were: William, Prince of Denmark, becomes George I, King of Greece. The French captures Mexico City and proclaims Arch duke Maximilian of Austria the emperor. First International Workingmen's Association is founded by Karl Marx. Bismarck and Napoleon III meet in Biarritz. Some current authors were Wilkie Collins, George Eliot, Charles Dickens, Dostoyevsky, Charles Kingsley, Tolstoy, Anthony Trollope, Lewis Carroll, Mary Mapes Dodge, Mark Twain, and Walt Whitman. Louis Pasteur develops germ theory of fermentation; invents pasteurization for wine; succeeds in curing silkworm disease, thus saving the French silk industry. Speed of light was sucessfully measured. Johann von Lamont discovers earth currents. Germany's botanist, Julius Sachs, demonstrates that starch is produced by photosynthesis. Ebenezer Butterick develops first paper dress patterns. Atlantic cable is completed. Joseph Lister initiates antiseptic surgery by using carbolic acid on a compound wound. Henri Dunant proposes the foundation of an international voluntary relief organization (the Red Cross). Football Association is founded in London. Grand Prix de Paris has its first run. William Booth establishes the Christian Revival Association (the Salvation Army).

2. This assignment allows your student the opportunity to participate in an interview, note taking, and writing.

Activities

The following activities are designed to help you increase your enjoyment of *Across Five Aprils*. Choose as many of the activities as you desire. Complete the activities on a separate piece of paper.

1. What important events were taking place in the world during the time of the Civil War?

2. Many of the events related in this story were told to the author by her grandfather. This is known as oral history. Although your grandfather was not alive during the time of the Civil War, he or another older person you know has many stories they can tell you. Ask him what he witnessed in his youth. You may record his stories for others to read.

3. Education was very important to Jethro and his family. His education took place in a one room schoolhouse as well as at home. Today, most children attend public schools. Trace how our education system came to be this way.

4. Read a biography of one of the historical figures mentioned in the book, such as Lincoln, Grant, Lee, or Sherman.

5. Aside from the slavery issue, the Civil War was fought over the issue of secession, the North wanting to keep the states united and the South desiring to separate and govern themselves. Do you think unity was important? Should the South have been allowed to secede? Write a short paper explaining your position.

6. When Jethro had a problem with the government's policy regarding deserters, he decided to write a letter to the president explaining the problem and asking for a reply. Write a letter to the president asking him a question or stating your views.

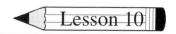

"Ye have heard that it hath been said, 'Thou shalt love thy neighbor and hate thine enemy.' But I say unto you, Love your enemies, bless them that curse you, do good to them that hate you, and pray for them which despitefully use you and persecute you; that ye may be the children of your Father which is in heaven: for he maketh his sun to rise on the evil and on the good, and sendeth rain on the just and the unjust."

Matthew 5: 43-45 (KJV)

✐ **Teacher's Note:** As your student completes each lesson, choose skills from the *Review Activities* that he needs. The *Review Activities* follow each lesson.

1. a. The literature passage which you will write from dictation today is taken from the King James Version of the Bible. Some of the words are not used in our language today. Listen carefully as your teacher dictates.

   b. Compare your work with the model and make any necessary corrections. If you misspelled any words, add them to your *Personal Spelling List*.

   c. Take a spelling test of the next ten words from the *Commonly Misspelled Words List*. Add the ones you miss to your *Personal Spelling List* and study the list this week.

   d. Make a list of words from the literature passage that are out of use today, such as *hath*. What words would we use instead?

   e. Begin memorizing the literature passage. Be ready to write or say it from memory on Day 5.

2. a. Vocabulary Builder - despitefully, persecute

   Write a dictionary sounding definition for the words *despitefully* and *persecute* using the context clues and your own knowledge. Try checking the *Word Parts Lists* in the *Appendix* for additional help. Now look up these words in the *Glossary*. Write a sentence using each word.

   b. Remember that **synonyms** are words that have similar meanings. **Antonyms** are words that have opposite meanings. Find and circle the four pairs of antonyms in the literature passage.

1.
d. Ye - You
   hath - has
   thou - You
   thy - your
   thine - your
   unto - to
   maketh - makes
   sendeth - sends

2.
a. *despitefully* - with violent hatred

   persecute - to pursue in a manner to injure

b. love - hate
   bless - curse
   evil - good
   just - unjust

2.

c.

1) love - to have a strong affection or personal attachment; syn: affection, fondness, warmth, devotion, esteem, regard

2) hate - to regard with a strong dislike; Syn: abhor, loathe, abominate, despise, detest

3) enemy - someone who harbors hatred or harmful designs against another Syn: antagonist, adversary, foe

4) neighbor - one who lives near another; Syn: fellow citizen

5) bless - to bestow good of any kind upon; Syn: praise, exalt, honor, extol

6) curse - the expression of a wish that evil would befall another; Syn: blast, denounce, abuse, plague

7) persecute - to pursue with harassment or oppressive treatment; Syn: torture, abuse, afflict, torment, bully, annoy

8) evil - one who violates the moral law; Syn: villain, criminal, wrongdoer, sinner, offender

9) good - morally excellent; Syn: pure, moral, virtuous, conscientious

10) just - actuated by truth, justice, and lack of bias; Syn: upright, fair, impartial

11) unjust - not acting fairly; Syn: unfair, partial, prejudiced, wrong

3.

b. Answer on p. 55 margin.

4.

a. Answer on p. 55 margin.

c. Write a brief definition for these words used in the literature passage. Next, use your thesaurus and find synonyms for these words. Save your work for tomorrow.
1) love
2) hate
3) enemy
4) neighbors
5) bless
6) curse
7) persecute
8) evil
9) good
10) just
11) unjust

d. Continue your memorization of Matthew 5:43-45.

3. a. Optional: If you have various Bible versions available, read Matthew 5:43-45 in a different version.

b. paraphrase - Greek παραφρασις: παρα - para - beyond
ρασις - phrasis - phrase

A **paraphrase** is a restating of a text of passage (going beyond the phrase) in words that follow the sense of the author but not the exact words. Today you will write a paraphrase of this week's literature passage. Use your own words, but stay close to its original meaning. The definitions and synonyms you looked up yesterday will help you. If you had opportunity to read the Scripture in another version, that will also help.

c. Continue your memorization.

4. a. Turn to Lesson 2 and read the literature passage about "The Good Samaritan" again. Compare the behavior of the Samaritan to Jesus' teaching in Matthew 5. To **compare** two things, you point out the similarities. Discuss this with your teacher, and write a paragraph.

b. This week's literature passage is part of Jesus' Sermon on the Mount found in Matthew 5-7. This is the best known sermon ever preached. The theme is discipleship. Read the sermon.

c. Can you think of a time when someone wasn't fair or kind to you? Maybe you were able to apply the teaching in Matthew 5:43-45. Perhaps you didn't. Write about what happened. If you didn't apply this teaching, what could you have done differently? Write about this.

d. Continue your memorization.

5. a. Take a spelling test of the words you misspelled this week.

b. Optional: On a separate piece of paper, take the literature passage from dictation again.

c. Recite Matthew 5:43-45 from memory, or write it on a separate piece of paper.

d. Choose skills from the *Review Activities* on the next page.

3.

b. Possible answer: You have heard that you should love your neighbor and hate your enemy. But I say, love your enemies, and be good and kind to them. Pray for those who mistreat you so that you may truly be God's children. God makes the sun to rise and the rain to fall on both the good and evil person.

4.

a. Possible answer: Although the Samaritans were not friendly with the people of the stranger, the Samaritan actively loved his "enemy." He could have left the stranger to die, but he chose to "love" him.

Review Activities

Choose skills your student needs to review.

1. *Paraphrase*
   Paraphrase these verses:

   Two things I asked of Thee,
   Do not refuse me before I die:
   Keep deception and lies far from me,
   Give me neither poverty nor riches;
   Feed me with the food that is my portion,
   Lest I be full and deny Thee and say
   "Who is the Lord?"
   Or lest I be in want and steal
   And profane the name of my God.

2. *Synonyms and Antonyms*
   Write a synonym and an antonym for each of these words:

   a. deception
   b. poverty
   c. riches
   d. full
   e. want
   f. steal
   g. profane

---

1. Lord, there are two things I would like for You to do for me. Please grant these requests while I am alive. First, do not let me practice deceit or lying. Second, do not let me become excessively poor or rich. Give me just enough food. Because if I have too much and would not acknowledge You. I would not know You. And if I am poor and have great need I may steal. That would disgrace Your name.

2.

Synonym	Antonym
a. deceit	honesty
b. privation	affluence
c. wealth	dearth
d. packed	empty
e. deficiency	plenty
f. purloin	supply
g. blaspheme	reverence

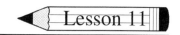

"He was only a tame old lion," said Jane impatiently, "and why are people making such a fuss over it?"

"Jane, my adored Jane, for the sake of your poor father's nerves, don't go leading any more lions about the country, tame or otherwise."

"But it's not a thing that's likely to happen again, Dad," said Jane reasonably.

Jane of Lantern Hill by L. M. Montgomery

1. a. Write the literature passage from dictation. First, if you are not sure how to put quotation marks (" ") around the words someone speaks, read the selection first and note how quotation marks are used.

   b. Compare your copy with the model and make the necessary corrections. If you misspelled any words, add them to your *Personal Spelling List*.

   c. Take a spelling test of the next ten words from the *Commonly Misspelled Words List*. Add any words you miss to your *Personal Spelling List* and study the list this week.

   d. Read the literature passage out loud trying to speak as you think each person would.

   e. There are five words in the literature passage that have an apostrophe ('). Write each word and indicate if it is a possessive noun or a contraction. If a contraction, write the two words it represents. If it indicates possession, tell who possesses what.

2. a. Vocabulary Builder - impatiently

   Write a dictionary sounding definition for the word *impatiently* using the context clues and your own knowledge. The *Word Parts Lists* could be of help also. Now look up the word in the *Glossary*. Write a sentence using this word correctly.

✎ **Teacher's Note: As your student completes each lesson, choose skills from the *Review Activities* that he needs. The *Review Activities* follow each lesson.**

1.
e. don't - contraction - do not

   father's - possessive - nerves belonging to father

   don't - contraction - do not

   it's - contraction - it is

   it's - contraction - it is

2
a. not patiently

2.

b. Jane

a different person

A new paragraph begins every time the speaker changes.

c.

Rule 1. All of the sentences are enclosed with quotation marks.

Rule 2. "He was only..." "Jane, my adored Jane...." "But it's not a thing..."

Rule 3. "He was only a tame old lion," said Jane impatiently, "and why are....it?"

Rule 4. ...old lion," ...over it?" ...otherwise." ....Dad,"

Rule 5. The second paragraph indicates a change in speaker from Jane to Father. The third paragraph indicates a change in speaker from Father to Jane.

d. Answers will vary.

3.

a. tame, old

adjectives

b. your

---

b. Who is speaking in the first paragraph of the literature passage? Is the second paragraph spoken by the same person or a different person? How can you tell?

c. Read the following *Quotation Rules*, and find an example of each of the rules in the literature passage.

Quotation Rules
1) Use quotation marks to enclose a person's exact words spoken or thought.
2) Begin a direct quotation with a capital letter.
3) When a quoted sentence is divided into two parts (split quotation), begin the second part with a small letter.
4) A period, comma, exclamation mark, or question mark following a quotation is placed inside the closing quotation marks.
5) Begin a new paragraph every time the speaker changes.

d. Using correct punctuation, write a short conversation you have had today.

3. a. Look at the first sentence of the literature passage. What words describe the kind of lion Jane led? What kind of words describe nouns or pronouns?

b. In the second paragraph of the literature passage, Jane is called "my adored Jane." *My* and *adored* are adjectives modifying the proper noun *Jane*. *My* is a possessive pronoun. What is the other possessive pronoun used in the literature passage?

c. Words that modify verbs are called **adverbs**. Adverbs also modify other adverbs and adjectives. Just as adjectives make nouns and pronouns more specific, adverbs make verbs, adjectives, and other adverbs clearer.

Adverbs answer three types of questions.
    Time: When? How Often?
    Place: Where?
    Manner: How? How Much?

Many adverbs are formed from adjectives by adding the suffix **-ly**. Find the two adverbs that tell you how Jane spoke.

Hint
Most words ending in **-ly** are adverbs. Careful, some words are adjectives, such as *friendly* and *lovely*.

d. Adjectives usually come before the noun or pronoun they modify. However, adverbs often appear after the verbs they modify, although they can appear anywhere in a sentence.

Underline the adverbs in these sentences from *Jane of Lantern Hill* and tell which question they answer.
1) So, in spite of everything, Jane went very happily through the gates of sleep.
2) Her hands were suddenly clammy but her mouth was dry.
3) For the first time Jane could join in the singing of the hymns, and she did it lustily.
4) The storm broke presently and lasted for two days.
5) Grandmother wiped her lips daintily with her napkin.

3.
c. impatiently
   reasonably

d.
  1) So, in spite of everything, Jane went <u>very</u> <u>happily</u> through the gates of sleep. (how much) (how)
  2) Her hands were <u>suddenly</u> clammy but her mouth was dry. (when)
  3) For the first time Jane could join in the singing of the hymns, and she did it <u>lustily</u>. (how)
  4) The storm broke <u>presently</u> and lasted for two days. (when)
  5) Grandmother wiped her lips <u>daintily</u> with her napkin. (how)

3.
e. 1) sa untered, strolled, etc.
2) shouted, bellowed, etc.
3) ached, throbbed, etc.
4) gobbled, devoured, etc.
5) scrutinized, probed, etc.

4.
a. Answers will vary.

b. Answers will vary.

5.
b. Answers will vary.

e. While adjectives and adverbs are very useful, they can be overused. As you develop your writing skills, strive to say what you want without using unnecessary words. Using a strong verb is often more effective than using the adverb-verb combination.

For instance, instead of writing "he spoke softly," you could write "he whispered" or "he muttered." Practice choosing strong verbs by changing these adverb-verb combinations to a single verb. This can be difficult. Use your thesaurus if you need help by looking up the base form of the verb.
1) walked slowly _____
2) talked loudly _____
3) hurt badly _____
4) ate quickly _____
5) looked closely _____

4. a. Use each of the following adverbs in a sentence.
   1) often
   2) happily
   3) finally
   4) down
   5) extremely
   6) loudly

   b. The literature passage records a very unusual conversation between a father and daughter. What might have happened before this conversation took place? Write what you think could have happened.

5. a. Take a spelling test of the words you misspelled this week.

   b. Read the literature passage in Lesson 4. What do you think Sara might have replied to Lavinia? Write what she might have said as a quote and use proper punctuation.

c. Write sentences from *Jane of Lantern Hill* as your teacher dictates them to you. Underline the adverbs used and tell what question they answer.
1) Mrs. Kennedy was perfectly satisfied with 60 Gay Street.
2) Jane walked slowly to prolong the pleasure.
3) Occasionally there was a line that gave her a thrill.
4) Jane fairly gritted her teeth.
5) At sunset, Jane and Dad went down to the outside shore.

d. Optional: On a separate piece of paper, take the literature passage from dictation.

e. Choose skills from the *Review Activities* on the next page.

5.
c. 1) perfectly (how)
2) slowly (how)
3) occasionally (when or how often)
4) fairly (how)
5) down (where)

Review Activities

Choose skills your student needs to review.

1. *Adverbs*
   Copy these sentences adding an adverb in the blank space.

   a. Chicken Little pecked _____ in the garden.
   b. _____, a rose leaf fell on her tail.
   c. She clucked _____ because she thought the sky was falling.
   d. Chicken Little _____ told everyone what she thought.
   e. Her foolishness _____ cost her her life.

2. *Punctuation / Quotations*
   Copy the following literature passage from *Jane of Lantern Hill* and add the correct punctuation for dialogue:

   We must get a cow said Justina. She must have a glass of warm milk every night at bedtime. We must furnish the little southwest room for her said Violet. I think I should like a carpet of pale blue, Sister. She must not expect to find here the excitements of the mad welter of modern life said Justina solemnly, but we shall try to remember that youth requires companionship and wholesome pleasures.

---

1. Possible answers:
   a. contentedly
   b. Suddenly
   c. hysterically
   d. quickly
   e. certainly

2. "We must get a cow," said Justina. "She must have a glass of warm milk every night at bedtime."

   "We must furnish the little southwest room for her," said Violet. "I think I should like a carpet of pale blue, Sister."

   "She must not expect to find here the excitements of the mad welter of modern life," said Justina solemnly, "but we shall try to remember that youth requires companionship and wholesome pleasures."

✏ Teacher's Note: The word *Sister* is capitalized in the literature passage because it is used as a name.

✏ Teacher's Note: Check for new paragraphs for each new person speaking.

It has been said that the whale only breathes through his spout-hole; if it could truthfully be added that his spouts are mixed with water; then I opine we should be furnished with the reason why his sense of smell seems obliterated in him; for the only thing about him that at all answers to his nose is that identical spout-hole; and being so clogged with two elements, it could not be expected to have the power of smelling. But owing to the mystery of the spout - whether it be water or whether it be vapor - no absolute certainty can as yet be arrived at on this head. Sure it is, nevertheless, that the sperm whale has no proper olfactories. But what does he want of them? No roses, no violets, no Cologne-water in the sea.

Moby Dick by Herman Melville

Teacher's Note: As your student completes each lesson, choose skills from the *Review Activities* that he needs. The *Review Activities* follow each lesson.

1. a. Write the literature passage from dictation. Compare your copy to the model. Make corrections. If you misspelled any words, add them to your *Personal Spelling List.*

   b. Take a spelling test of the next ten words from the *Commonly Misspelled Words List.* If you miss any, add them to your *Personal Spelling List* and study them throughout the week.

   c. Vocabulary Builder - opine, obliterated, olfactories

   Write a dictionary sounding definition for the words *opine, obliterated,* and *olfactories,* using context clues and your own knowledge. Can you gain any clues by looking at the *Word Parts Lists*? Now look up these words in the *Glossary* to see if you were right. Write a sentence using each word.

1.
c. *opine* - to think
   obliterated - erased
   olfactories - organs pertaining to smelling

Points to Ponder

Cologne, most oftenly seen as "eau de cologne" means water of Cologne. Cologne is a city in Germany. We very often use the words *cologne* or *perfume* for any scented liquid, but originally perfumed toilet water was made in the German city of Cologne in 1709, hence the name. This is why Cologne is capitalized in this literature passage, even though we now use it to name any perfumed toilet water.

Why "toilet" water? The word *toilet* comes from the French word, *toile,* meaning cloth. A cloth was usually spread over a table in a chamber or dressing room. The word began to be used to name the dressing table and then to include the whole room.

2. a. Adverbs modify verbs, adverbs, and adjectives. They can appear almost anywhere in a sentence. In fact, they can even be moved around within the sentence without changing the meaning of the sentence. For example, in the dependent clause "if it could truthfully be added that his spouts are mixed with water," the adverb is *truthfully* telling how it could be added. *Truthfully* could be placed in any position within the clause:

> *truthfully* if it could be added…
> if *truthfully* it could be added…
> if it *truthfully* could be added…
> if it could *truthfully* be added…
> if it could be *truthfully* added…
> if it could be added *truthfully*…

Most of these sound fine. Some are awkward, but they all work.

2
a. **Possible Answer:**
1) Little Red Riding Hood skipped <u>happily</u> through the woods.
2) <u>Soon</u> she met a wolf.
3) The wolf <u>quickly</u> made his way ahead of Little Red Riding Hood.
4) Little Red Riding Hood <u>obediently</u> approached her Grandma's bed.
5) Little Red Riding Hood called for help <u>loudly</u>.
6) The wolf ran <u>away</u>.

Because of this flexibility, adverbs are sometimes hard to identify. Place the following adverbs in the sentences where you think it sounds best:

1) (happily) Little Red Riding Hood skipped through the woods.
2) (soon) She met a wolf.
3) (quickly) The wolf made his way ahead of Little Red Riding Hood.
4) (obediently) Little Red Riding Hood approached her grandma's bed.
5) (loudly) Little Red Riding Hood called for help.
6) (away) The wolf ran.

b. The first sentence of the literature passage is very long, making it a little hard to follow. Rewrite this sentence into three to four sentences using different punctuation.

c. Is the last line in the literature passage a complete sentence? What is the definition of a complete sentence? As you have learned in Lesson 4, authors sometime intentionally use incomplete sentences for emphasis or effect. Use this sparingly in your writing.

d. Write the last line of the literature passage as a complete sentence.

3. a. There are two basic kinds of verbs: action verbs and linking verbs. Action verbs are words that suggest physical or mental activity. Make a list of the action verbs in the literature passage.

b. **Linking verbs** connect (link) the subject of a sentence to a related noun, pronoun, or adjective in the predicate. Linking verbs express a state of being because they help describe or identify a person or thing. The verb *be* is the most common linking verb. It has many forms: *am, is, was, were, be, being*, and *been*. Circle the linking verbs in the literature passage.

2.
a. **Answers on p. 64 margin**

b. **Possible answer:
It has been said that the whale only breathes through his spout-hole. If it could truthfully be added that his spouts are mixed with water, then I opine we should be furnished with the reason why his sense of smell seems obliterated in him. For the only thing about him that at all answers to his nose is that identical spout-hole. Being so clogged with two elements, it could not be expected to have the power of smelling.**

c. **No. A sentence is a group of words, containing a subject and a predicate, which express a complete thought.**

d. **Possible answers:
There are no roses, no violets, no Cologne-water in the sea. Or The sea does not contain any roses, violets, or Cologne-water.**

3.
a. **said, breathes, added, mixed, opine, furnished, obliterated, clogged, expected, can, arrived, want**

b. *is* **that identical spout-hole**
be **furnished**
has **no proper olfactories**

3.

c. Possible answers:
1) I *feel* fine today.
   The fur *feels* soft.
2) John will *grow*
   tomatoes.
   The tree *grows* tall.
3) I will *look* for my pen.
   She *looks* beautiful.
4) The weather *seems* to
   be changing.
   The man *seems*
   confident.
5) The alarm will *sound*
   loudly.
   The story *sounds*
   interesting.
6) I will *taste* the soup.
   The pie *tastes*
   delicious.

d. could *(not)* be expected

e. But what *does* he *want*
   of them?

c. Some verbs can be used as either linking or action verbs.
   Ex: Susan *smells* the soup. (action)
   The soup *smells* delicious. (linking)

   Write two sentences using the following verbs. Use the verbs as an action verb and then as a linking verb:
   1) feel
   2) grow
   3) look
   4) seem
   5) sound
   6) taste

d. You have circled the action verbs and the being verbs in the literature passage. There is one more group of verbs in the literature passage. A verb may consist of more than one word. A verb with more than one word is called a **verb phrase**, consisting of the main verb and one or more helping verbs. A **helping verb** helps the verb express action or make a statement. Being verbs may also be used as helping verbs.

Being Verbs
am   is   are   was
were   be   being   been

Helping Verbs			
have	has	had	do
does	did	may	might
must	can	could	shall
should	will	would	

Sometimes the verb phrase will be broken up by another word. One common interrupter is the word *not* or the contraction *n't*. *Not* and *n't* are never part of the verb. Find an example of a verb phrase interrupted by *not* in the literature passage.

Hint
The words *not* and *n't* are adverbs.

e. Verb phrases in questions are often interrupted by the subject. Find an example of this in the literature passage.

f. In **2a**, we have already learned that adverbs can also interrupt a verb phrase. Find another example of this in the literature passage.

g. Find the verbs in the literature passage in Lesson 6. Indicate if they are action, linking, or helping verbs.

4. a. Points to Ponder

   Moby Dick is considered one of the great novels in American literature. Its author, Herman Melville, was born in 1819 to a wealthy family. When he was eleven years old, his father died and left the family in a poor financial state. Melville spent the early part of his adult life on merchant and whaling ships where he had many adventures. After a short stint in the Navy, Melville returned home. Using his wealth of experience and a vivid imagination, he began to write.

   b. One of the most important rules for a writer is to write about what he knows. Herman Melville followed this rule. In this week's literature passage, he shares some of his knowledge gained while serving on whaling ships.

   Look up sperm whales in an encyclopedia, science book, or reference book and find out some information about their spout-hole and how they breathe. Is Mr. Melville's information correct?

   c. Write a paragraph paraphrasing what you have learned. Remember, to paraphrase what you have read, you rewrite it in your own words.

3.
f. being *so* clogged

g. fell (action)
   showed (action)
   were (linking)
   had (linking)
   would have (helping)
   caused (action)
   had (helping)
   been (linking)
   were (linking)
   looked (action)
   lay (action)
   showed (action)

4.
b. Some facts you will find:
   Sperm whales are mammals that can grow to 60 feet long and weigh up to 60 tons.
   Whales have lungs. They must come to the surface to breathe.
   Sperm whales can hold their breath up to 75 minutes.
   Whales' muscles store more oxygen than other mammals.
   Humans store only about 13 percent oxygen, while whales store about 41 percent.
   Whales breathe through nostrils called blowholes or spout-holes located on the tops of their heads.
   A cloud called a blow or spout is produced when a whale exhales. It consists of water vapor.
   A sperm whale's blow can be up to 25 feet.

5.

c. Possible answers:
   1) swiftly, quietly, etc.
   2) Softly, Stealthily, etc.
   3) loudly, clearly, etc.
   4) easily, carefully, etc.
   5) jauntily, quickly, etc.
   6) Then, Soon, etc.
   7) too, terribly, etc.
   8) truly, really, etc.
      extremely, always, etc.

d. wore (action)
   had been (helping)
   piled (action)
   had been (helping)
   fashioned (action)
   was (helping)
   garnished (action)
   were (helping)
   decorated (action)
   was (linking)
   would (helping)
   form (action)
   was (linking)

5. a. Take a spelling test of the words you misspelled this week.

b. Optional: On a separate piece of paper, take the literature passage from dictation again.

c. Add adverbs to these sentences to make them more vivid.
   1) Curious George climbed _____ into the window of the house.
   2) _____ he ran towards the tempting bike.
   3) The man in the yellow hat called after him _____.
   4) George didn't stop but climbed _____ on the bike.
   5) He waved _____ as he sped by.
   6) _____ he ran into the hedge.
   7) George was not _____ hurt.
   8) He was _____ sorry he was _____ curious.

d. Find the verbs in the literature passage in Lesson 1. Indicate if they are action, linking, or helping verbs.

e. Choose skills from the *Review Activities* on the next page.

Review Activities

Choose skills your student needs to review.

1. *Verbs*
Copy this literature passage from *Moby Dick*. Underline the verbs.

   I stuffed a shirt or two into my old carpetbag, tucked it under my arm, and started for Cape Horn and the Pacific. Quitting the good city of old Manhattan, I duly arrived in New Bedford. It was on a Saturday night in December. Much was I disappointed upon learning that the little packet for Nantucket had already sailed, and that no way of reaching that place would offer, till the following Monday.

2. *Action Verb, Linking Verb, Helping Verb*
Make a list of the verbs from the literature passage above, and indicate if they are action, linking, or helping verbs.

3. *Adverbs*
Circle the adverbs.

1. and 2.
- stuffed (action)
- tucked (action)
- started (action)
- quitting (action)
- arrived (action)
- was (linking)
- was (linking)
- had (helping)
- sailed (action)
- would (helping)
- offer (action)

3. duly, already

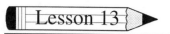

✏ **Teacher's Note:** As your student completes each lesson, choose skills from the *Review Activities* that he needs. The *Review Activities* follow each lesson.

Immortal, invisible God only wise,
In light inaccessible hid from our eyes,
Most blessed, most glorious, the Ancient of Days,
Almighty, victorious, Thy great name we praise.

Unresting, unhasting, and silent as light,
Nor wanting, nor wasting, Thou rulest in might;
Thy justice like mountains high soaring above
Thy clouds, which are fountains of goodness and love.

To all, life Thou givest, to both great and small;
In all life Thou livest, the true life of all;
We blossom and flourish as leaves on the tree,
And wither and perish - but naught changeth Thee.

"Immortal, Invisible, God Only Wise" by Walter Chalmers Smith

1. a. Listen as your teacher reads this poem. This is a hymn you may have sung in church. Write the poem from dictation. Often in poetry, each line begins with a capital letter even if it does not begin a sentence.

   b. Correct your copy and add any words you misspelled to your *Personal Spelling List.*

   c. Take a spelling test of the next ten words from the *Commonly Misspelled Words List.* If you miss any, add them to your *Personal Spelling List* and study the list throughout the week.

   d. If you know this hymn, sing it.

2. a. Vocabulary Builder - inaccessible, immortal, flourish

Write a dictionary sounding definition for these words using the context clues and your own knowledge as well as any other clues you can find in the *Word Parts List*. Now look up the words in the *Glossary*. Write a sentence using each word.

b. In the literature passage from Lesson 1, the author described a familiar scene by appealing to our sense of sight. Some things are difficult to describe without comparing them to something more familiar. Figurative language is used to do this. **Figurative language** helps create associations for the reader to better aid his understanding.

The most commonly used figures of speech are similes and metaphors. Both of these make associations between two dissimilar things. A **simile** does this by using the words *like* or *as*.
Ex: silent *as* light

Find two more similes in this hymn.

c. A **metaphor** also finds a likeness between two dissimilar things, but doesn't use the words *like* or *as*. Metaphors make the association by stating that one *is* the other. Find the metaphor in this hymn.

d. Read the following poem. Find an example of figurative language, either simile or metaphor, and underline it.

The same leaves over and over again!
They fall from giving shade above
To make one texture of faded brown
And fit the earth like a leather glove.

(Robert Frost)

e. Memorization is a great exercise for the brain. Begin memorizing "Immortal, Invisible, God Only Wise." You will write it from memory on Day 4.

2.

a. *inaccessible* - not able to be reached
immortal - never ending
flourish - to thrive

b. Thy justice <u>like</u> mountains

We blossom and flourish <u>as</u> leaves on a tree

c. Thy clouds, which are fountains of goodness and love.

d. fit the earth <u>like</u> a leather glove (simile)

71

3. a. God

God is immortal.
God is invisible.
God is the only wise one.
God is hidden from our eyes.
God is the most blessed.
God is the most glorious.
God is eternal (Ancient of Days).
God is almighty.
God is victorious.
God does not need to rest.
God is never in a hurry.
God has no needs.
God does not waste anything.
God's justice is over all.
God covers us with goodness and love.
God is the giver of life.
God is unchanging.

b. Possible answers: The only wise God is immortal. He is invisible to our eyes. We praise and bless the name of the most glorious Ancient of Days. He is almighty and always victorious. God does not need to rest or to hurry. He has no needs and everything he does has a purpose. He rules over all the earth, etc.

c. wise, eyes
Days, praise
light, might
above, love
small, all
tree, Thee

d. invisible, inaccessible
glorious, victorious
unhasting, wasting
mountains, fountains
givest, livest
flourish, perish

3. a. In the hymn "Immortal, Invisible, God Only Wise" whom is the writer describing? Make a list of truths about God, which the poet expresses.
Ex: God is immortal.

b. The ordinary form of speaking or writing is called **prose** as opposed to poetry which has a metrical structure and is expressed in verses. Write this hymn in prose.

c. Not all poetry is written in rhyme, but virtually all songs do have a rhyming pattern. In this hymn the words at the end of the lines rhyme. Write the pairs of rhymes.

d. Not only are there rhymes at the end of the lines, but there are also **internal rhymes**, words within the lines that rhyme. Can you find these pairs?

e. Continue your memorization.

4. a. Write "Immortal, Invisible, God Only Wise" from memory.

b. Think of some attributes of God. Write two to three similes comparing God's attributes to something else.
Ex: God's love abounds like the endless sky.

c. Write two to three metaphors comparing God's attributes.
Ex: His faithfulness is a fortress.

5. a. Take a spelling test of words you misspelled this week.

b. How well did you memorize the hymn yesterday? Recite it to your teacher today.

c. A good use of simile and metaphor should surprise the reader and help give new insight. Some similes have been used so often they have lost the quality of surprise. They are called **cliches**. It is hard to think of good, fresh similes and metaphors, especially when you are talking. As a writer you can take the time to think of a good comparison.

Practice by writing a simile for the following:
1) fragile as _____
2) squeaky as _____
3) red as _____
4) fast as _____

Now try these:
5) The clown laughed like _____.
6) Shari's eyes shone like _____.
7) The baby crawled like _____.

d. Similes are usually easier to spot than metaphors because of the use of *as* or *like*. In a metaphor the thing compared is stated as if it actually were the thing it is compared to. For example, in Psalm 119 we read, "Thy Word is a light unto my path." Written as a simile this would read: Thy word is *like* a light unto my path.

Write two metaphors of your own.

4.
b. Answers will vary.

c. Answers will vary.

5.
c. Possible answers
   1) **a butterfly wing**
   2) **a nagging woman**
   3) **Rudolph's nose**
   4) **lightning**
   5) **a hyena**
   6) **stars**
   7) **a turtle**

d. Answers will vary.

Review Activities

1. peace like a river
   sorrow like sea billows
   clouds as a scroll

2. Possible answer: You have taught me to be content no matter what happens to me, good or bad. I look forward to the day when the Lord shall return to Earth. Then, even as before, I will be content.

3. A Mighty Fortress is our God
   A Bulwark never failing

1. *Similes*
   Underline the similes in this hymn by Horatio G. Spafford:

   When peace like a river attendeth my way,
   When sorrow like sea billows roll,
   Whatever my lot,
   Thou hast taught me to say,
   It is well, it is well with my soul.

   And Lord haste the day when my faith shall be sight
   The clouds be rolled back as a scroll.
   The trump shall resound
   And the Lord shall descend
   Even so, it is well with my soul.

2. *Prose*
   Write the hymn in prose.

3. *Metaphors*
   Underline the metaphors in this hymn by Martin Luther.

   A Mighty Fortress is our God,
   A Bulwark never failing
   Our helper He amid the flood
   Of mortal ills prevailing.
   For still our ancient foe
   Doth seek to work us woe;
   His craft and power are great,
   And, armed with cruel hate,
   On earth is not his equal.

The Moat House stood not far from the rough forest road. Externally, it was a compact rectangle of red stone, flanked at each corner by a round tower, pierced for archery and battlemented at the top. Within, it enclosed a narrow court. The moat was perhaps twelve feet wide, crossed by a single drawbridge. It was supplied with water by a trench, leading to a forest pool and commanded, through its whole length, from the battlements of the two southern towers. Except that one or two tall and thick trees had been suffered to remain within half a bowshot of the walls, the house was in a good posture for defense.

The Black Arrow by Robert Louis Stevenson

1. a. Write the literature passage from dictation. Compare your copy with the model and make corrections as needed. If you misspelled any words, add them to your *Personal Spelling List* and study them this week.

   b. Take a spelling test of the next ten words from the *Commonly Misspelled Words List*. Add any you miss to your *Personal Spelling List* and study them this week.

   c. Review the *Comma Rules* found in the *Appendix* at the back of the book. Commas help make writing clearer and easier to read.
   Ex: Within it enclosed a narrow court. (unclear)
       Within, it enclosed a narrow court. (clear)

   d. Look at the literature passage. What is the antecedent for the pronoun *it* in "it was a compact rectangle"? What is the antecedent for *it* in "it was supplied with water by a trench"?

2. a. Vocabulary Builder - flanked, battlement, battlemented, posture

   Write a dictionary sounding definition for each of these words using the context clues and your own knowledge. Now look up these words in the *Glossary*. Write a sentence for each word.

✎ Teacher's Note: As your student completes each lesson, choose skills from the *Review Activities* that he needs. The *Review Activities* follow each lesson.

1.
d. the Moat House
   the moat

2.
a. *flanked* - bordered
   battlement - an upper wall
   battlemented - secured by battlements
   posture - situation

2.
b. (The) Moat House
   stood

   <u>from the rough forest
   road</u>

b. Read the first sentence of the literature passage. What is the subject? What is the verb? *Not* is a special kind of adverb that makes the adverb *far* negative. Underline the remaining words in the first sentence.

c. The phrase you underlined, "from the rough forest road," is called a prepositional phrase. A **prepositional phrase** begins with a preposition followed by a noun or pronoun which often has modifiers. **Prepositions** show the relation of a noun or pronoun with another word in the sentence. The preposition *from* shows the relation of *stood* to the *rough forest road.*

Commonly Used Prepositions				
aboard	at	except	on	toward
about	before	for	onto	under
above	below	from	out	underneath
across	beneath	in	outside	until
after	beside	inside	over	unto
against	between	into	past	up
along	but	like	since	upon
among	by	near	through	with
around	down	of	throughout	within
as	during	off	to	without

d. Circle all the prepositions in the literature passage.

d. from, of, at, by, for, at,
   by, with, by, to, through,
   from, of, within, of, in,
   for

e. Make a list of the prepositions found in the literature passage in Lesson 1.

e. of, of, for, along, into,
   with, of, with, of, In, in, of,
   of

f. In order to see how prepositions change the relationship between words, copy the sentences below and choose three appropriate prepositions to fill in the blank. Choose prepositions that will make sense in the sentence.

Ex: She planted her garden _____ (*around, behind, near*) the old tree.

f. Possible answers:
   1) after, before, during
   2) against, behind,
      beside
   3) at, after, during
   4) toward, past, beyond
   5) in, within, at

1) Cinderella scrubbed the floor _____ dinner.
2) She stood _____ the carriage.
3) She met the Prince _____ the ball.
4) The servant carried the slipper _____ her.
5) Cinderella and the Prince were happy _____ the castle.

3. a. A preposition *never* stands alone in a sentence. It always has a noun or pronoun as its object. The **object** of the preposition almost always comes after the preposition. In sentences introduced by an interrogative pronoun (who, whose, whom, which, and what) or a relative pronoun (who, whose, whom, which, what, that, whoever, whatever, whichever), the object can appear before the preposition. Circle the nouns that follow the prepositions you circled in **2d**.

   b. Underline the words that appear between the prepositions and their objects you circled. These should all be adjectives modifying the object of the preposition. All the words from the circled preposition to the circled object is called the prepositional phrase.

   c. Many of the words that act as prepositions can also be used as other parts of speech. Remember, in order for a word to act as a preposition, it *must* have an object. Often, when a word that looks like a preposition does not have an object, it is an adverb. Indicate if the italicized words in the following sentences from *The Black Arrow* are prepositions or adverbs.
   1) The path went *down into* the marsh.
   2) They were free *of* the passage.
   3) A torch lit *up* the scene.
   4) The moon had gone *down*.
   5) Sentinels were posted close *around* the house and garden.

   d. In the last sentence of the literature passage, there is a word that sometimes acts as a preposition but it is not one here because it does not have an object. Can you find it?

   The word *to* in this context is used as part of an infinitive, a verb form. We will discuss this further in Lesson 21.

4. a. Draw a diagram of the Moat House and its surroundings using the description found in the literature passage. Put everything in your picture.

   b. Why do you think it was important for the defense of the house that there were few trees nearby?

3.
a. road, stone, corner, tower, archery, top, drawbridge, water, trench, pool, length, battlements, towers, bowshot, walls, posture, defense

b. the rough forest, red, each, a round, the, a single, a, a forest, its whole, the, the two southern, half a, the, a good

c.
1. down (adverb)
   into (preposition)
2. of (preposition)
3. up (preposition)
4. down (adverb)
5. around (preposition)

d. (to remain)is a verb form

4.
b. Anyone approaching the house would be in full view and without protection.

    c. In Lesson 1, you wrote a description of a familiar scene. In Lesson 6, you wrote a description of a person. Today you will write a description of a familiar place, perhaps your room, your church, or a favorite park. Use prepositional phrases to clarify your description.

5. a. Take a spelling test of the words you misspelled this week.

    b. Using the description you wrote in **4c**, draw a diagram of the place you described. Did you have enough detail?

    c. If possible, on a separate piece of paper have someone else draw a diagram of the place using your description. Does he think you need more detail?

    d. Go through the description you wrote in **4c**, and circle the prepositions and underline their objects.

    e. Choose skills from the *Review Activities* on the next page.

Review Activities

Choose skills your student needs to review.

1. *Prepositions, Object of the Preposition, Adjectives*
   Copy this literature passage from *The Black Arrow*:

   On a certain afternoon, in the late springtime, the bell upon Tunstall Moat House was heard ringing at an unaccustomed hour. Far and near, in the forest and in the fields along the river, people began to desert their labours and hurry towards the sound; and in Tunstall hamlet a group of poor country folk stood wondering at the summons.

   a. Circle all the prepositions and box in the object of each preposition.

   b. Underline the adjectives in the prepositional phrases. Include articles.

1.
a. Prepositions: On, in, upon, at, in, in, along, towards, in, of, at

Objects: afternoon, springtime, Tunstall Moat House, hour, forest, fields, river, sound, hamlet, folk, summons

b. Adjectives: a certain, the late, an unaccustomed, the, the, the, the, Tunstall, poor country, the

Teacher's Note: As your student completes each lesson, choose skills from the Review Activities that he needs. The *Review Activities* follow each lesson.

"Well, goodness me! I can't see anythin' ter be glad about—gettin' a pair of crutches when you wanted a doll!"

Pollyanna clapped her hands.

"There is—there is," she crowed. "But I couldn't see it, either, Nancy, at first," she added, with quick honesty. "Father had to tell it to me."

"Well, then, suppose **you** *tell* **me***," almost snapped Nancy.*

"Goosey! Why, just be glad because you **don't***—need—'em!" exulted Pollyanna triumphantly.*

Pollyanna by Eleanor H. Porter

1. a. Listen as your teacher reads the literature passage out loud.

   b. Review the *Quotation Rules* listed in Lesson 11.

   c. Write the literature passage from dictation. Compare with the model and correct. Add any misspelled words to your *Personal Spelling List*.

   d. Take a test of the next ten words from the *Commonly Misspelled Words List*. Add any words you misspell to your *Personal Spelling List* and study the list this week.

2. a. Vocabulary Builder - honesty, exulted, triumphantly

   Write a dictionary sounding definition for these words using any context clues and your own knowledge to help you. Now look up these words in the *Glossary*. Write a sentence for each of these words.

2.

a. *honesty* - truth
   exulted - rejoiced
   triumphantly - in a victorious manner

b. Circle the words the author chose to misspell in the
    literature passage. Why do you think she wrote this way?
    Language can vary from region to region and usage can
    also change. Still, there are certain standards of writing
    English that are considered appropriate. This is called
    Standard English. Standard English consists of both formal
    and informal English. Formal English is what is most often
    used in serious writing and speaking. Informal English is
    more often used in everyday situations. Nonstandard
    English is what is used in this paragraph. It would not be
    suitable for formal or informal writing because of the stigma
    it carries.

c. Read the literature passage out loud replacing the words
    with Formal English. Does it change the literature passage
    in any way?

d. Underline the verbs that describe how Pollyanna or Nancy
    said something.
    Ex: she <u>crowed</u>

    Read the literature passage out loud replacing the underlined
    words with *said*. Do you like the way it sounds?

e. *Said* is the past tense of the verb *say*. Look up *say* in your
    thesaurus and make a list of ten synonyms for this word.

f. *She crowed* or *he said* are called **speech tags**. There are two
    points of view about using speech tags. There is the *said*
    camp which feels that great variety in speech tags is
    distracting to the reader. The other camp feels that *said* is
    repetitious and monotonous. But one point is agreed in both
    camps: Use speech tags only as needed to clarify the person
    who is speaking. You might want to experiment with these
    two techniques. Replace the synonyms for *said* in this
    passage with *said*. Which do you like better?

2.

b. anythin'
   ter'
   gettin'
   'em

   **Nancy is a servant and
   in this period of time
   would not have
   had much education.**

c. anything
   to
   getting
   them

**d. crowed, snapped,
   exulted**

**e. Possible answers:
   utter, pronounce,
   articulate, reply, state,
   declare, mention, cry,
   breathe, add**

3. a. **Dialogue**, what people say, makes a story more interesting to read. For example, read the following dialogue from *Pollyanna*:

Pollyanna found her aunt in the sitting room.

"Who was that man—the one who drove into the yard, Pollyanna?" questioned the lady a little sharply.

"Why, Aunt Polly, that was Dr. Chilton! Don't you know him?"

"Dr. Chilton! What was he doing—here?"

"He drove me home. Oh, and I gave the jelly to Mr. Pendleton and—"

Miss Polly lifted her head quickly.

"Pollyanna, he did not think I sent it?"

"Oh, no, Aunt Polly. I told him you didn't."

Miss Polly grew a sudden vivid pink.

"You *told* him I didn't?"

Pollyanna opened wide her eyes at the remonstrative dismay in her aunt's voice.

"Why, Aunt Polly, you *said* to!"

Aunt Polly sighed.

"I *said*, Pollyanna, that I did not send it, and for you to be very sure that he did not think I *did*—which is a very different matter from *telling* him outright that I did not send it." And she turned vexedly away.

Now read how this scene would be told by a narrator:

Pollyanna found her aunt in the sitting room. Her aunt asked her who had driven into the yard. Pollyanna told her it was Dr. Chilton. Her aunt wanted to know what he was doing there. Pollyanna told her he had driven her home.

She then told her aunt she had given the jelly to Mr. Pendleton. Her aunt interrupted her to ask if he had thought she, Aunt Polly, had sent it. Pollyanna said she knew he hadn't because she told him Aunt Polly had not.

Aunt Polly was dismayed to hear this. Pollyanna told her she thought that was what Aunt Polly had wanted. Aunt Polly explained that she had only meant that she didn't want Mr. Pendleton to *think* she had sent it which is a very different thing from telling him so. Aunt Polly was very bothered.

Good books have a variety of narration and dialogue.

b. Using the following narration of a well-known fairy tale, add dialogue to tell the story.

3.
b. Answers will vary. Be sure your student has included dialogue and speech tags (where necessary), and indented correctly.

Papa Bear, Mama Bear, and Baby Bear sat down to breakfast, but found the porridge was too hot to eat, so they decided to go for a walk.

A little girl named Goldilocks, who was wandering in the forest, came upon their cottage and knocked on the door and called out. When no one answered, Goldilocks tried the door and, finding it open, went in. She saw the bowls of porridge and tasted each one. Her comments about it was that one was too hot, one was too cold, and one was just right. She ate the just right bowl.

She went into the sitting room and saw three chairs. Upon trying them out, she found that one was too hard, one was too soft, and one was just right. She sat in the just right one and rocked and rocked until it suddenly broke under her.

She was so tired by that time that she went upstairs to the bedroom where she found three beds. The first one was too hard, the second one was too soft, but the small one was just right. She climbed in the just right one and fell fast asleep.

About this time, the bears decided it was time to come back home. When they came in they found the porridge had been disturbed. They discussed what to do and decided to check out the rest of the house. They were shocked to discover the broken chair. Discussing this situation they decided to continue their search of the house.

They went upstairs and were surprised to find Goldilocks asleep in Baby Bear's bed. They woke her up and asked what she thought she was doing. Goldilocks explained what had happened and ask their forgiveness for intruding. The bears forgave Goldilocks and they parted friends.

c. Think of a conversation you had today. If you cannot remember exactly what was said, supply words needed to convey the meaning. You may choose to attach speech tags, but remember to use them only as needed.

4. Another excellent way to practice writing dialogue is to conduct an interview. Choose a specific topic and interview someone you know. You could ask your parents about how they met, ask your grandparents what school was like when they were young, or ask your neighbor what he remembers about his first job.

Interview Guidelines

1) *Before the interview*, think about your topic and write down questions to ask.
2) *During the interview*, write down only the important phrases the person says. You might find having a portable tape recorder would be helpful for reference when you start writing.
3) *As soon as you can*, write out your notes.

You should be ready now to write a report of your interview. Write an **introductory paragraph** describing the person you are interviewing, perhaps the setting where the interview took place, or the reason for the interview. Then write a dialogue of the interview.
Ex:

"Pastor Brown," I began, "What main event led you to consider going into the ministry?"

"That's easy," he replied. "I remember sitting in a small country church on a cold November evening, listening to my father preach, as I had many times before, when I suddenly felt a strange warming in my heart."

5. a. Take a spelling test of the words you misspelled this week.

b. Write this week's literature passage as a narration.

c. Who is your favorite character in history? Conduct an imaginary interview today with that person and record the conversation. Refer to the *Interview Guidelines*.

d. Complete the *Review Activities*, if needed.

5.
b. Possible answer:
    Nancy told Pollyanna that she couldn't see anything to be glad about —getting a pair of crutches when you wanted a doll.
Pollyanna clapped her hands and told her that at first she couldn't see it either, but her father explained it to her. Nancy wanted to know, so Pollyanna told Nancy that she should be glad just because she didn't need them.

Review Activities

The following is a narrated version of a conversation between Pollyanna and a gentleman. Write it as a dialogue. Experiment with speech tags.

The gentleman wanted to know why Pollyanna didn't find someone her own age to talk to. Pollyanna said she would like to, but there weren't any around. She didn't mind so very much because she likes old folks just as well, maybe better, sometimes. She was used to the Ladies' Aid.

The gentleman was indignant! Is that what she took him for? There was a smile threatening on his lips, but the scowl above them was still trying to hold them grimly stern. Pollyanna laughed gleefully.

She told him he did not look at all like a Ladies' Aider, although he was just as good, maybe better. She told him that he was much nicer than he looked.

This is how the author wrote the passage, but expect your student's work to be somewhat different.

"See here, why don't you find someone your own age to talk to?"

"I'd like to, sir, but there aren't any around here, Nancy says. Still, I don't mind so very much. I like old folks just as well, maybe better, sometimes—being used to the Ladies' Aid, so."

"Humph! The Ladies' Aid indeed! Is that what you took me for?" The man's lips were threatening to smile, but the scowl above them was still trying to hold them grimly stern.

Pollyanna laughed gleefully.

"Oh, no, sir. You don't look a mite like a Ladies' Aider—you're just as good, of course—maybe better," she added politely. "You see, I'm sure you're much nicer than you look!"

✎ **Teacher's Note:** As your student completes each lesson, choose skills from the *Review Activities* that he needs. The *Review Activities* follow each lesson.

On the 3rd of October the army of Cromwell appeared in sight. In the city, Edward had been on horseback, attending the King for the best part of the night; the disposition of the troops had been made as well as it could; and it was concluded, as Cromwell's army remained quiet, that no attempt would be made on that day. About noon, the King returned to his lodging to take some refreshment after his fatigue. Edward was with him; but before an hour had passed the alarm came that the armies were engaged. The King mounted his horse, which was ready saddled at the door; but before he could ride out of the city he was met and nearly beaten back by the whole body almost of his own cavalry, who came running on with such force that he could not stop them.

The Children of the New Forest by Frederick Marryat
(Captain Marryat)

1. a. Write the literature passage from dictation. Compare with the model and make corrections.

   b. Take a review spelling test of words your teacher chooses from your *Personal Spelling List*.

   If you misspelled any words from your dictation, add them to your *Personal Spelling List* and study them this week. Add any other words you misspell your *Personal Spelling List* and study them during the week.

   c. In the first prepositional phrase of the literature passage "on the 3ʳᵈ," *3ʳᵈ* is an ordinal number acting as a noun. Since *The Children of the New Forest* was written 150 years ago, writing rules were different than they are today. It is customary today to write out the word for *3ʳᵈ* as *third*. The number would be used if the date were written like this: on October 3.

2. a. Vocabulary Builder - disposition, fatigue, engaged, cavalry

   Write a dictionary sounding definition for these words, using the context clues and your previous knowledge along with any help you can get from the *Word Parts List*. Then look up the definitions in the *Glossary*. Write a sentence for each word.

   b. Circle the four semicolons (**;**) used in the literature passage. Read each of the clauses separated by these semicolons. Are they independent clauses (complete sentences) or dependent clauses (a group of words that cannot stand alone as a complete thought)?

   c. Read the following *Semicolon Rules*.

   ### Semicolon Rules

   1) Semicolons are usually used to connect independent clauses that are *not* joined by a conjunction.
   Ex: I smelled the crisp morning air; fall had finally arrived.

   2) Semicolons are used to separate independent clauses joined by transitional phrases such as *for example* or *in fact*.
   Ex: Today was a hot day; in fact, it was a record breaker.

   3) Semicolons are sometimes used instead of a comma to separate groups of items in a series to add clarity.
   Ex: Be prepared for your camping trip. Bring a hat, jacket, and boots; matches, flashlight, and knife; water bottle, fruit, and nuts.

   Although rules do exist, the use of semicolons is often a stylistic decision of a writer, primarily used to vary the length of sentences. Read the paragraph out loud stopping at the semicolons as if they were periods and leaving out any conjunctions such as *and* or *but*. Compare it to the original. Which do you think sounds better?

   d. Look at the second sentence in the literature passage. Which number rule applies to the use of the semicolon in this sentence?

2.
a. *disposition* - temperament
fatigue - exhaustion of strength
engaged - entered into conflict with
cavalry - a body of military troops on horses

b. ...part of the night (dependent clause);

... it could (independent clause);

... with him (independent clause);

... the door (dependent clause)

d. night; the disposition - Rule 1

could; and it was concluded - Rule 2

3.

a. *Twice Freed*
  A Tale of Two Cities
  The Black Arrow

3.

c. 1) **Cromwell's army appeared (flashback)**
2) **Edward had been on horseback most of the night. (flashback)**
3) **The disposition of troops had been made. (flashback)**
4) **The King returned to his lodgings for nourishment about 12:00 noon.**
5) **Edward was with him. Within an hour the alarm was sounded that the armies were fighting.**
6) **The King mounted his horse.**
7) **Before he could ride out of the city, he was met and driven back by his own cavalry.**
8) **He could not stop them.**

3. a. *The Children of the New Forest* is an example of a **historical fiction**. The story is set in a real time and place in history and some of the characters actually lived. Of the literature passages you have read, three books would be considered historical fiction. Can you name them?

b. *The Children of the New Forest* is set in a time of Civil War in England. Look in the encyclopedia or other resource to find more information about this period of English history. You may begin by looking up Oliver Cromwell and King Charles. This information will help you understand the background to this historical fiction.

c. You have learned about descriptive writing (Lessons 1, 6, and 13) and persuasive writing (Lesson 7). This week's literature passage is an example of **narrative writing**. Narration is a type of writing used to tell a story or relate an event. Like descriptive writing, narrative writing requires vivid and interesting details.

A narrative paragraph records events in a sequence which should lead the reader to question, "What happens next?" The events are usually told in chronological order; that is, in the order they occurred in time. Sometimes the order is interrupted by a flashback to give important information that occurred earlier. The second sentence in the literature passage is a flashback. Then the paragraph proceeds in chronological order.

Make a list of things that happened in this story.
Ex: Cromwell's army appeared.
    Edward had been on horseback most of the night. (flashback)

d. Use your list to tell the story to your teacher. Improve the list if you find it didn't help enough in telling the story.

4. a. Today you will write a narrative paragraph. Think of an event in your life, perhaps your last birthday or family vacation. You might tell of the time you broke your arm or of some project you have completed. Write about what happened using the following guidelines to help you.

Guidelines in Narrative Writing

1) When writing events that occur in a sequence, use transitional words that help the reader follow the sequence, such as *first, second, before, earlier, then, next*, or *last*. Do not overuse any of these words.

2) Use specific nouns and strong action verbs.
   Ex: The teenager drove away in his car. (*Car* is a general noun.)
   The teenager drove away in his convertible. (*Convertible* is a specific noun which gives a clearer picture.)

---

5. a. Take a spelling test of the words you misspelled this week.

   b. Read the story you wrote in **4a**. Does it follow a chronological sequence? Did you choose specific nouns and strong action verbs? Revise your story as needed.

   c. Using the list of events you recorded on **3c**, write the story in your own words without looking at the model.

   d. Choose skills from the *Review Activities* on the next page.

Review Activities

1. *Semicolon - Independent Clause*
Join the following sentences using a semicolon.

   a. The girls went biking.
      The boys went skating.
   b. My scuba diving lessons start tomorrow.
      I can hardly wait.
   c. Joe got his driver's license.
      He's coming in ten minutes.

2. *Semicolon - Transitional Words*
Join the following sentences using a semicolon and a transitional word or phrase.

   a. We tried to be on time.
      We were late.
   b. You're never too old to learn.
      Grandma Moses began painting in the later years of her life.
   c. Mom was constantly baking during the holidays.
      I gained ten pounds.

3. *Semicolon - series*
Add commas and semicolons.

The manager asked me to play with the kittens puppies and bunnies wash disinfect and line the cages and sweep mop and wax the floors.

1.
a. The girls went biking; the boys went skating.
b. My scuba diving lessons start tomorrow; I can hardly wait.
c. Joe got his driver's license; he's coming in ten minutes.

2. Possible answers:
a. We tried to be on time; however, we were late.
b. You're never too old to learn; for example, Grandma Moses began painting in the later years of her life.
c. Mom was constantly baking during the holidays; as a result, I gained ten pounds.

3. The manager asked me to play with the kittens, puppies, and bunnies; wash, disinfect, and line the cages; and sweep, mop, and wax the floors.

Assessment 2
(Lessons 10 - 16)

1. Read these two verses of a hymn written by Manie P. Ferguson, and underline the similes.

Joys are flowing like a river,
Since the Comforter has come.
He abides with us forever,
Makes the trusting heart His home.

Like the rain that falls from heaven,
Like the sunlight from the sky,
So the Holy Ghost is given,
Coming on us from on high.

2. Write the first simile as a metaphor.

3. Write the hymn in prose.

4. Write two antonyms and two synonyms for each of these words:

   a. joy
   b. comfort
   c. come
   d. trust
   e. high

---

1. Joys are flowing like a river
   The Holy Ghost is given like the rain that falls from heaven and like the sunlight from the sky

2. Joys are a flowing river

3. Possible answer:
   Joy surrounds us and fills us since the Holy Spirit has been given to us. He lives in our hearts and will never leave us. God has sent His Holy Spirit to us just as He has given us all good things.

4. Possible answers:
   Synonyms
   a. *joy* - delight, rapture
   b. *comfort* - solace, reassure
   c. *come* - approach, appear
   d. *trust* - faith, reliance
   e. *high* - lofty, towering

   Antonyms
   a. *joy* - sorrow, despair
   b. *comfort* - distress, torment
   c. *come* - depart, leave
   d. *trust* - doubt, disbelief
   e. *high* - low, reduced

5. "What made him speak so sharply to you, Edward?" asked Humphrey.

"Because he means kindly, but does not want other people to know it, " replied Edward. "Come in, Humphrey; I have much to tell you and much to surprise you with."

"I have been surprised already," replied Humphrey. "How did this roundhead know Clara's father so well?"

"I will explain all before we go to bed, " replied Edward. "Let us go in now."

6. asked Humphrey
replied Edward
replied Humphrey
replied Edward

7.
a. <u>cautiously</u> (advanced)
b. <u>immediately</u> (assented)
c. <u>humbly</u> (answered); <u>only</u> (had been)
d. <u>very</u> (severe); <u>very</u> (heavy)

8. when, how often, where, how, how much

9. *Cautiously,* they advanced into the thicket.
They *cautiously* advanced into the thicket.
They advanced *cautiously* into the thicket.
They advanced into the thicket *cautiously.*

Immediately Edward assented.
Edward *immediately* assented.
Edward assented *immediately.*

---

5. Copy the following literature passage taken from *The Children of the New Forest*. Insert the correct punctuation for dialogue:

What made him speak so sharply to you, Edward, asked Humphrey.

Because he means kindly, but does not want other people to know it replied Edward Come in, Humphrey; I have much to tell you and much to surprise you with.

I have been surprised already replied Humphrey How did this roundhead know Clara's father so well?

I will explain all before we go to bed replied Edward Let us go in now.

6. Underline the speech tags used in the above passage.

7. Underline the adverbs in the following sentences from *The Children of the New Forest*. Tell what word each adverb modifies.

a. They advanced cautiously into the thicket.
b. Edward immediately assented.
c. He answered humbly, observing that he had only been doing his duty.
d. The winter set in very severe, and the falls of snow were very heavy and frequent.

8. What questions to adverbs answer?

9. Rewrite sentences **7a** and **b** above, placing the adverb differently each time.

10. Make a list of prepositional phrases found in this literature passage from *The Black Arrow*:

   Dick's heart smote him at what he heard. Until that moment he had not perhaps thought twice of the poor skipper who had been ruined by the loss of the *Good Hope*; so careless, in those days, were men who wore arms of the goods and interests of their inferiors. But this sudden encounter reminded him sharply of the high-handed manner and ill-ending of his enterprise; and both he and Lawless turned their heads the other way, to avoid the chance of recognition.

11. Circle the prepositions and underline their objects.

12. Make a list of the action verbs found in the literature passage in exercise 10. If any of the action verbs contain helping verbs, put parentheses around the helping verbs.

13. Using your verb list from above, write the infinitive, present participle, past, and past participle for each verb.

---

10. at what

   Until that moment

   of the poor skipper

   by the loss

   of the *Good Hope*

   in those days

   of the goods and interests

   of their inferiors

   of the high-handed manner and ill-ending

   of his enterprise

   of recognition

11. (at) what
    (Until) moment
    (of) skipper
    (by) loss
    (of) *Good Hope*
    (in) days
    (of) goods, interests
    (of) inferiors
    (of) manner, ill-ending
    (of) enterprise
    (of) recognition

12. smote, heard, (had) thought, (had been) ruined, reminded, turned

13. Answers on bottom of this page.

Answers:

13.

Infinitive	Present Participle	Past	Past Participle
smite	smiting	smote	(have) smote
hear	hearing	heard	(have) heard
think	thinking	thought	(have) thought
ruin	ruining	ruined	(have) ruined
remind	reminding	reminded	(have) reminded
turn	turning	turned	(have) turned

14. Possible answer:
I don't think the written word could ever compare to something created, like a tree. A tree that sends its roots down deep into the earth to receive water and nourishment. A tree that stands in God's sight with her branches stretching toward heaven as if in prayer. A tree that is a home to the birds of the air. A tree who lives very close to nature. Man can do many things with words but God is the only one who can create life.

14. Write a paraphrase of this poem by Joyce Kilmer:

I think that I shall never see
A poem lovely as a tree.

A tree whose hungry mouth is pressed
Against the earth's sweet flowing breast;

A tree that looks at God all day
And lifts her leafy arms to pray;

A tree that may in summer wear
A nest of robins in her hair;

Upon whose bosom snow has lain;
Who intimately lives with rain.

Poems are made by fools like me,
But only God can make a tree.

BOOK STUDY

on

A Lantern in
Her Hand

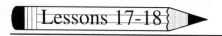
A Lantern in Her Hand
By Bess Streeter Aldrich
Published by Penguin
Group

Summary

Because the road was steep and long,
And through a dark and lonely land,
God set upon my lips a song
And put a lantern in my hand.

(Joyce Kilmer)

The year is 1868, as Will and Abbie Deal, along with their young son, cross over into the unsettled state of Nebraska. They are joined by other adventurous, dream-seeking people who hope to find a prosperous future in the rich soil. Many hard years are to follow as they struggle to maintain a foothold in the new land. Fighting drought and locust they stubbornly carve out a state of the Union. After much hard work and personal sacrifice, Abbie begins to see her dreams come true, but not quite the way she thought they would.

Unlike Laura Ingalls Wilder who tells her pioneer stories through the eyes of a child, Bess Streeter Aldrich gives us the mother's view of pioneer life. Her character, Abbie Deal, represents much of what was good about the early pioneers. She is long-suffering and possesses a strong love of family as well as a sense of duty to her family and her country.

Bess Streeter Aldrich's parents emigrated to the Iowa frontier in the 1850's. Bess was born in 1881 in Cedar Falls, Iowa and died in 1954 in Lincoln, Nebraska. After her marriage to Charles Aldrich in 1907, Mrs. Streeter wrote children's stories and also for teachers' magazines. Upon the sudden death of her husband in 1925, she became the sole supporter of her children and began writing full time.

In her first novel, *The Rim of the Prairie*, she demonstrated her ability to accurately and precisely describe the Midwest. *A Lantern in Her Hand* is probably her best work and is based on actual events, many of which her mother experienced.

Vocabulary

Find the word in its context. Reread the sentences before and after the word. What do you think the word means? Look up the word in the dictionary and write a clear, simple definition, and use it in a sentence.

1. martyred - (pg. 53)

2. colossal - (pg. 85)

3. replica - (pg. 117)

4. assuaged - (pg. 150)

5. intrigue - (pg. 221)

Complete the sentences with the correct vocabulary word. OR Write your own sentences using the vocabulary words.

6. The customer's anger was _____ after the manager explained the situation.

7. Courageous men and women were _____ for their faith.

8. John wants to study programming because computers _____ him.

9. The jeweler made a _____ of my grandmother's ring.

10. The _____ buildings loomed over the city.

1. persecuted for one's belief
2. huge
3. a reproduction
4. calmed or lessened
5. to excite the interest of

6. assuaged

7. martyred

8. intrigue

9. replica

10. colossal

Activities

Increase your enjoyment of this inspiring story by completing two or three of the following activities. Complete the activities on a separate piece of paper.

1. Begin making weekly visits to a nursing home. Try to draw out some oral histories of what life was like years ago for these people.

2. Abbie Deal lived through three wars: the Civil War, the Spanish American War, and War World I. Research the one least familiar to you.

3. Identify character qualities that were needed for the early pioneers. Do people still need these today, or are other qualities more important? Why or why not?

4. Look at old photograph albums. Note the changes in hair styles, clothes, automobiles, etc.

5. "How queer people were. All the folks in the new country were hoarding things, hanging onto old heirlooms...Sarah Lutz had a painting...Oscar Lutz's wife had a pink quilted bedspread...Even Christine Reinmueller had a bright blue vase with magenta colored roses on it...She must hang onto the pearls and everything they stood for." Does your family have a special family heirloom? Find out its history and write it down.

6. Go browsing in an antique shop. Ask the proprietor to explain some of the more unusual items and how they were used.

7. Abbie lived through an amazing time of new inventions: moving pictures, automobiles, radios, airplanes. Research the origin of these and add the dates to a timeline.

8. If you have read the Little House books by Laura Ingalls Wilder, make comparisons with the two pioneer families as you read *A Lantern in Her Hand*. How were their experiences similar? How did they differ?

9. "You <u>have</u> to dream things out. It keeps a kind of an ideal before you. You see it first in your mind and then you set about to try to make it like the ideal. If you want a garden, - why I guess you've got to <u>dream</u> a garden." Can you remember a time when this was true for you?

10. If you enjoyed reading *A Lantern in Her Hand*, read *The Rim of the Prairie*.

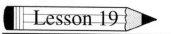

Teacher's Note: As your student completes each lesson, choose skills from the *Review Activities* that he needs. The *Review Activities* follow each lesson.

The Rainy Day

The day is cold, and dark, and dreary;
It rains, and the wind is never weary;
The vine still clings to the moldering wall,
But at every gust the dead leaves fall,
And the day is dark and dreary.

My life is cold, and dark, and dreary;
It rains, and the wind is never weary;
My thoughts still cling to the moldering Past,
But hopes of youth fall thick in the blast,
And the days are dark and dreary.

Be still, sad heart! and cease repining;
Behind the clouds is the sun still shining;
Thy fate is the common fate of all,
Into each life some rain must fall,
Some days must be dark and dreary.

Henry Wadsworth Longfellow

1. a. Listen as your teacher reads the poem. Write the poem from dictation. Compare with the model and make corrections. Add any misspelled words to your *Personal Spelling List.*

   b. Take a spelling test of the next ten words from the *Commonly Misspelled Words List* and add any words you misspell to your *Personal Spelling List.* Study the list this week.

   c. Read the poem out loud using good expression.

2. a. Vocabulary Builder - moldering, repining

   Write a dictionary sounding definition for each of these words using the context clues and your own knowledge. Now look up the words in the *Glossary.* To show you understand the words write a sentence using each word.

2.

a. *moldering* - turning to dust
repining - feeling discontent

b. Poems that rhyme, such as "The Rainy Day," usually follow a pattern. This pattern is known as the **rhyme scheme**. To determine the rhyme scheme, a letter is assigned to the lines that end in the same rhyme. Look at the sample poem that follows.

Twinkle, twinkle little star (**a**)
How I wonder what you are (**a**)
Up above the world so high (**b**)
Like a diamond in the sky. (**b**)

The rhyme scheme of "Twinkle, Twinkle" is **aabb**.

Note: The rhyme scheme may not be consistent throughout a poem.

c. Read the following poem and analyze its rhyme scheme.

2.
c. abba

Friend of my many years!
When the great silence falls, at last, on me,
Let me not leave, to pain and sadden thee,
A memory of tears,

But pleasant thoughts alone
Of one who was thy friendship's honored guest
And drank the wine of consolation pressed
From sorrows of thy own.

I leave with thee a sense
Of hands upheld and trials rendered less—
The unselfish joy which is to helpfulness
Its own great recompense;

The knowledge that from thine,
As from the garments of the Master, stole
Calmness and strength, the virtue which makes whole
And heals without a sign;

Yea more, the assurance strong
That love, which fails of perfect utterance here,
Lives on to fill the heavenly atmosphere
With its immortal song.

(John Greenleaf Whittier)

2.
d. aabba

e. life
Because we live in a fallen world, we all will experience sad, hard times. We should not be discouraged by them.

3.
b. Máry hád a líttle lámb
His fléece was whíte as snow,
And éverywhére that Máry wént
The lámb was súre to go.

c. stressed, unstressed (trochaic)

---

d. Analyze the rhyme scheme of "The Rainy Day" using the model.

e. Discuss the poem with your teacher. To what is Longfellow comparing a rainy day? What lesson is Longfellow teaching?

3. a. In Lesson 4, **4a**, you learned that writing has a rhythm. This is especially true for poetry. The rhythm of poetry can be analyzed by listening for stressed syllables. Read the following poem, noting the stressed syllables. Stress marks (**/**) indicate where to add stress in your voice.

   Twínkle, twínkle líttle stár
   Hów I wónder whát you áre
   Úp abóve the wórld so hígh
   Líke a díamond ín the ský.

   b. Add stress marks to "Mary Had a Little Lamb."

   Mary had a little lamb
   Its fleece was white as snow.
   Everywhere that Mary went
   The lamb was sure to go.

   c. When analyzing a poem's rhythm, the syllables of a line are heard in groups of two's or three's. In "Twinkle, Twinkle" and "Mary Had a Little Lamb" the first syllable of every two syllables is stressed, so the rhythm sounds like DUMM-de DUMM-de, etc. Each of these rhythmic unit is called a foot. **Foot** is a unit of meter which denotes the combination of stressed and unstressed syllables. These are the most common units of meter:

   iambic - unstressed, stressed (U /)
   anapestic - unstressed, unstressed, stressed (U U /)
   trochaic - stressed, unstressed (/ U)
   dactylic - stressed, unstressed, unstressed (/ U U)

   In what foot are "Twinkle, Twinkle" and "Mary Had Little Lamb" written?

d. Scan the following poem and determine its rhyme scheme and rhythmic foot.

> When Earth's last picture is painted, and the tubes are
>   twisted and dried,
> When the oldest colors have faded, and the youngest critic
>   has died,
> We shall rest, and, faith, we shall need it—lie down for an
>   eon or two,
> Till the Master of All Good Workmen shall set us to work
>   anew!
>
> And those who were good shall be happy: they shall sit in a
>   golden chair;
> They shall splash at a ten-league canvas with brushes of
>   comet's hair;
> They shall find real saints to draw from—Magdalene, Peter,
>   and Paul;
> They shall work for an age at a sitting and never be tired at
>   all!
>
> And only the Master shall praise us, and only the Master
>   shall blame;
> And no one shall work for money, and no one shall work
>   for fame;
> But each for the joy of the working, and each, in his
>   separate star,
> Shall draw the Thing as he sees It for the God of Things as
>   They Are!

(Rudyard Kipling)

Note: Poets take liberties with metrical patterns as well as rhyme schemes. Also, two readers may scan the same poem and have different opinions about the metrical pattern.

e. You probably have noticed that it is much easier to memorize something if you can sing it. One reason is because of the repetitious pattern of rhyme and meter. Memorize the poem "The Rainy Day."

3.
d. aabb, unstressed,
   stressed (iambic)

103

4.
a. for example: with a gulp,
and a pant, and a smile

b. dark and dreary; day is
dark and dreary; sun still
shining

c. Words with the long e
sound

4. a. **Alliteration** is the repeating of the same consonant sound at the beginning of words. Poetry especially is enhanced using alliteration. Most authors use some alliteration to add a pleasing rhythm to their writing. In Rudyard Kipling's *Captains Courageous*, we find this line:

...he swallowed the hint with a gulp and a gasp and a grin.

Substitute synonyms for one or two of the words beginning with **g**. Does it sound as good as the original?

b. Find examples of alliteration in "The Rainy Day." Underline them.

c. There are two other repetitious techniques frequently used by poets. The same vowel sounds may be repeated without repeating the consonants. This is called **assonance**. Underline examples of assonance in this poem:

The Vulture eats between his meals.
  And that's the reason why
He very, very, rarely feels
  As well as you or I.
His eye is dull, his head is bald.
  His neck is growing thinner
Oh, what a lesson for us all.
  To only eat at dinner.

d. **Consonance** is the repetition of consonant sounds not
limited to the first letter of each word. Underline examples
of consonance in this poem:

It isn't the thing you do, dear,
    It's the thing you leave undone
That gives you a bit of a heartache
    At setting of the sun.
The tender word forgotten,
    The letter you did not write,
The flowers you did not send, dear,
    Are your haunting ghosts at night.

The stone you might have lifted
    Out of a brother's way;
The bit of heartsome counsel
    You were hurried too much to say;
The loving touch of the hand, dear,
    The gentle, winning tone
Which you had no time nor thought for
    With troubles enough of your own.

Those little acts of kindness
    So easily out of mind,
Those chances to be angels
    Which we poor mortals find—
They come in night and silence,
    Each sad, reproachful wraith,
When hope is faint and flagging,
    And a chill has fallen on faith.

For life is all too short dear,
    And sorrow is all too great,
To suffer our slow compassion
    That tarries until too late;
And it isn't the thing you do, dear,
    It's the thing you leave undone
Which gives you a bit of a heartache
    At the setting of the sun.

(Margaret E. Sangster)

5.

c. Lesson 7 - ababddee
Alliteration - broad
stripes and bright stars;
rocket's red glare;
bombs bursting; star
spangled; wanting,
wasting

Lesson 13 - aabb
Alliteration - immortal,
invisible; unresting,
unhasting

d. <u>**with walls, fearless foot**</u>
<u>**deep, dividing**</u>
<u>**flows and foams**</u>
<u>**set sail**</u>
<u>**doors of daring**</u>
<u>**dare, die**</u>

e. Continue memorizing "The Rainy Day."

5. a. Take a spelling test of the words you misspelled this week.

b. Recite "The Rainy Day."

c. Scan the poems in Lessons 7 and 13. Determine their rhyme scheme. Look for alliteration, and underline it.

d. Read the following poem and underline examples of alliteration.

The mountains that inclose the vale
  With walls of granite, steep and high,
Invite the fearless foot to scale
  Their stairway toward the sky.

The restless, deep, dividing sea
  That flows and foams from shore to shore,
Calls to its sunburned chivalry,
  "Push out, set sail, explore!"

The bars of life at which we fret,
  That seem to prison and control,
Are but the doors of daring, set
  Ajar before the soul.

Say not, "Too poor," but freely give;
  Sign not, "Too weak," but boldly try;
You never can begin to live
  Until you dare to die.

(Henry van Dyke)

e. Choose skills from the *Review Activities* on the next page.

Review Activities

Choose skills your student needs to review.

1. *Rhyme Scheme*
   What is the rhyme scheme of this first verse of a poem by
   Theodosia Garrison?

   Because I craved a gift too great
   For any prayer of mine to bring,
   Today with empty hands I go;
   Yet must my heart rejoice to know
   I did not ask a lesser thing.

2. *Meter*
   What is its meter?

3. *Alliteration*
   Underline an example of alliteration in this poem by Isaac Watts:

   Let dogs delight to bark and bite,
   For God hath made them so;
   Let bears and lions growl and fight,
   For 'tis their nature too.

   But, children, you should never let
   Such angry passions rise;
   Your little hands were never made
   To tear each other's eyes.

1. abccb

2. unstressed, stressed
   (iambic)

3. <u>dogs delight</u>
   <u>bark and bite</u>

Lesson 20

Proverbs 6:6-11

✎ **Teacher's Note:** As your student completes each lesson, choose skills from the *Review Activities* that he needs. The *Review Activities* follow each lesson.

1.

c. poverty will come *like* a vagabond
your need *like* an armed man

d. By observing the ant's behavior, we can learn important lessons. A slothful person who will not work will not be able to provide for his own needs or take care of what he does have.

2.

a. *sluggard* - habitually lazy person
provision - supplies of food
vagabond - one who wanders from place to place

*Go to the ant, O sluggard, observe her ways and be wise, which, having no chief, officer or ruler, prepares her food in the summer, **and** gathers her provision in the harvest. How long will you lie down, O sluggard? When will you arise from your sleep? "A little sleep, a little slumber, a little folding of the hands to rest"— and your poverty will come in like a vagabond, and your need like an armed man.*

Proverbs 6:6-11 (NASB)

1. a. Write the literature passage from dictation. Compare with the model and make corrections. Add any misspelled words to your *Personal Spelling List.*

   b. Take a spelling test of the next ten words from the *Commonly Misspelled Words List.* Add any words you misspell to your *Personal Spelling List* and study the list during the week.

   c. The literature passage contains two similes. Underline them and tell your teacher what two things are being compared in each.

   d. Discuss the literature passage with your teacher. Why are we told "go to the ant"? Why will *poverty* and *need* come? What lesson is being taught?

2. a. Vocabulary Builder - sluggard, provision, vagabond

   Write a dictionary sounding definition for these words using the context clues and your own knowledge. Look up the words in the *Glossary* and then write a sentence for each one.

   b. Sentences are classified according to their purpose.

108

Types of Sentences

1) **Declarative sentences** make statements and are punctuated with a period (**.**).
   Ex: Declarative sentences make statements.

2) **Interrogative sentences** ask questions and are punctuated with a question mark (**?**).
   Ex: Do interrogative sentences ask questions?

3) **Exclamatory sentences** express strong emotion or surprise and are punctuated with an exclamation point (**!**).
   Ex: I cannot believe you wrote that exclamatory sentence!

4) **Imperative sentences** make a request or give a command and can be punctuated with either a period of an exclamation point.
   Ex: Punctuate that imperative sentence correctly.
   Ex: Punctuate that imperative sentence correctly!

c. The subject of an imperative sentence is usually the pronoun *you*.
   Ex: Go get a drink of water.
   (You) go get a drink of water.

You is not stated, but understood. This is true even if the person's name is stated.
Ex: Mary, go get a drink of water.
   Mary, (you) go get a drink of water.

Underline the imperative sentence in this week's literature passage.

2
c. **(You) go to the ant...**

2.
d. 1) Will you walk into my parlor? (interrogative)
2) The fly said she would not. (declarative)
3) How brilliant are your eyes! (exclamatory)
4) Step in one moment. (imperative)
5) The fly felt flattered and went in. (declarative)
6) She never came out again! (exclamatory)

e. You will arise from your sleep when?

f. go, observe, be, prepares, gathers, will lie, will arise, will come

d. Punctuate the following sentences and indicate if they are declarative (**Dec**), imperative (**Imp**), interrogative (**Int**), or exclamatory (**Exc**).
1) Will you walk into my parlor
2) The fly said she would not
3) How brilliant are your eyes
4) Step in one moment
5) The fly felt flattered and went in
6) She never came out again

e. The usual sentence pattern for declarative sentences is subject-verb. Interrogative sentences usually have a split verb with the subject in between the helping verb and the main verb. This sometimes makes it difficult to identify the verb. It may help to reword the sentence so that the subject comes first.
Ex: How long will you lie down, O Sluggard?
　　You, O Sluggard, will lie down how long?

Will lie is the verb phrase.

Note: *O Sluggard* simply renames the subject, *you.*

Rewrite the other interrogative sentence in the literature passage. Underline the subject once and the verb twice.

f. Underline the verbs in the literature passage.

3. a. The first verb you underlined in **2f** should have been *go*. The second underlined verb should have been *observe.* These are both action verbs. There are two kinds of actions verbs: transitive and intransitive.

Transitive verbs *transfer* the action to an object, a noun, or a pronoun. That is, they complete a sentence by telling who or what is affected by the action.
Ex: Moses struck the rock three times.

The action of striking is transferred to the rock.
Intransitive verbs do *not* need an object to complete the statement.
Ex: Linda sneezed.

Most action verbs can be transitive or intransitive depending on how they are used.
Ex: (transitive)   Jill *sang* the national anthem.
     (intransitive) Jill *sang* beautifully.

b. An easy test to determine if an action verb is transitive or intransitive is to ask the question *who* or *what* after the verb. Using the first sentence of the literature passage, state the verb and then ask *who* or *what*.
Ex: go who? (There is no answer, so *go* must be an intransitive verb.)
Observe what? ("Observe *her ways*" completes the statement so it must be a transitive verb.)

c. The answer to the question *who* or *what* will be a noun or pronoun. This object is called the **direct object** of the verb. Direct objects do not follow linking verbs and are *never* in a prepositional phrase.
Ex: Go to the ant.
Ant is not a direct object. It is the object of the preposition *to*.

Hint
A direct object *never* follows a linking verb and is *never* in a prepositional phrase.

d. Underline the direct objects in the literature passage in Lesson 1. Now, underline the direct objects in the literature passage in Lesson 5. Remember, the direct object will be a noun or pronoun. It may be preceded by adjectives. It will *not* be in a prepositional phrase. It will *not* follow a linking verb.

Note: An action verb may have more than one object.

4. a. What is the linking verb in the first sentence? It is followed by the adjective *wise*. It is a predicate adjective. **Predicate adjectives** follow a linking verb and modify the subject of a sentence.
Ex: The flower arrangement was very beautiful.
     Beautiful is a predicate adjective modifying *arrangement*.

3.
d. **Lesson 1**
   wore (what?) <u>an air</u>

   would form (what?) <u>a column</u>

   Lesson 5
   would reach (what?) the lower <u>plain</u>

   see (what?) <u>outskirts</u>

   could hear (what?) <u>crying</u>

4.
a. be

Direct objects and predicate adjectives are words or groups of words (when they have adjectives or adverbs) that complete a statement begun by a subject and verb. They are called **complements**. There is another complement that is similar to predicate adjectives.

A **predicate nominative** is a noun or pronoun that identifies or renames the subject of the sentence. It follows a linking verb.
Ex: A thesaurus is a valuable tool for writers.
Tool identifies or renames *thesaurus*.

4.
b. 1) Jack was a poor boy.
   (predicate nominative)
2) He sold his cow for some beans. (direct object)
3) Jack climbed the beanstalk that grew. (direct object)
4) He found a goose that laid golden eggs. (direct object)
5) Jack was very happy. (predicate adjective)
6) Jack was now a rich boy. (predicate nominative)

b. Underline the predicate adjective, predicate nominative, or direct object in each of the following sentences and tell what it is:
1) Jack was a poor boy.
2) He sold his cow for some beans.
3) Jack climbed the beanstalk that grew.
4) He found a goose that laid golden eggs.
5) Jack was very happy.
6) Jack was now a rich boy.

c. Today you will write a story that has the same **moral** as this week's literature passage, Proverbs 6:6-11. A moral of a story is the lesson that the main character learns.

You have practiced writing narratives. To do this, you paid close attention to sequence and detail. The purpose was to tell what happened. In story writing you will do the same thing, but will also tell <u>why</u> it happened. Just as in writing narrative, you need to use specific nouns and strong verbs as well as dialogue. In fact, you should bring all the skills you have practiced to this exercise.

Your story should have a short beginning that sets the scene (setting) and introduces the characters. The middle part will tell what the story is about (plot) and how your characters confront and deal with a conflict or problem (i.e. laziness). The end of your story will resolve the conflict.

Elements in a Story				
Setting	Characters	Plot	Conflict	Resolution

5. a. Take a spelling test of the words you misspelled this week.

   b. If you need more time, finish your story today.

   c. Find the predicate nominative in the literature passage in Lesson 1.

   d. Rewrite your story in dialogue form as for a play. Don't forget to include the actions of the characters and the setting of the story. The form should look like this:

   MOTHER: (*enters John's bedroom*) John, it is time to get up. You promised Dad you would mow the lawn today.

   JOHN: (yawning) I'm coming. I'm coming. (*John turns over and goes back to sleep.*)

   e. Choose skills from the *Review Activities* on the next page.

5.
c. It was <u>Inauguration Day</u>

Review Activities

Choose skills your student needs to review.

1. *Types of Sentences and Punctuation*
   Punctuate the following sentences and tell if they are declarative (**Dec**), imperative (**Imp**), interrogative (**Int**), or exclamatory (**Exc**).

   a. The city mouse asked the country mouse to visit him
   b. He cried, "What a beautiful place to see"
   c. Watch out for the cat
   d. Would the city mouse return the visit
   e. The city mouse wanted to go home
   f. Each mouse thought that his home was best
   g. Isn't that how it should be

2. *Transitive and Intransitive Verb; Direct Object*
   Circle the verb in each sentence. Is it transitive (**T**) or intransitive (**IT**)? If transitive, what is the direct object?

   a. The ants worked hard all summer.
   b. The grasshopper played his violin.
   c. Winter came.
   d. The ants had plenty to eat.
   e. The grasshopper begged for food.
   f. The next summer, the grasshopper put his violin aside to work.

1.

a. The city mouse asked the country mouse to visit him. (declarative)
b. He cried, "What a beautiful place to see!" (exclamatory)
c. Watch out for the cat! (exclamatory or imperative)
d. Would the city mouse return the visit? (interrogative)
e. The city mouse wanted to go home. (declarative)
f. Each mouse thought that his home was best. (declarative)
g. Isn't that how it should be? (interrogative)

2.

a. worked (intransitive)
b. played (transitive) violin
c. came (intransitive)
d. had (transitive) plenty
e. begged (intransitive)
f. put (transitive) violin

Dawn came, and daylight. The fire was burning low. The fuel had run out, and there was need to get more. The man attempted to step out of his circle of flame, but the wolves surged to meet him. Burning brands made them spring back. In vain he strove to drive them back. As he gave up and stumbled inside his circle, a wolf leaped for him, missed and landed with all four feet in the coals. It cried out with terror, at the same time snarling, and scrambled back to cool its paws in the snow.

White Fang by Jack London

✎ **Teacher's Note:** As your student completes each lesson, choose skills from the *Review Activities* that he needs. The *Review Activities* follow each lesson.

1. a. Take the literature passage from dictation. Compare with the model and make corrections. Add any words you misspelled to your *Personal Spelling List.*

   b. Take a test of the next ten words from the *Commonly Misspelled Words List.* Add any you miss to your *Personal Spelling List* to be studied this week.

   c. Vocabulary Builder - brands

   Write a dictionary sounding definition for this word using the context clues and your own knowledge. Look it up in the *Glossary* and then write a sentence using the word.

   d. Nouns are usually made plural by adding **s** to the base word. Find an example of this in the literature passage. Not all nouns are made plural in this way.

   e. Read the following *Plural Rules.*

1.
c. *brands* - burning pieces of wood

d. brands, coals, paws

115

Plural Rules

1) To most nouns, just add **s**.
   Ex: chairs, phones, boys

2) To nouns ending in **s**, **sh**, **ch**, **z**, and **x**, add **es**.
   Ex: kiss - kisses; ash - ashes; bunch - bunches; buzz - buzzes; box - boxes;

3) To nouns ending in a consonant and **y**, change the **y** to **i** and add **es**.
   Ex: daisy - daisies

4) To nouns ending in a vowel and **y**, just add **s**.
   Ex: monkey - monkeys

5) To most nouns ending in a vowel and **o**, just add **s**.
   Ex: studio - studios

6) To most nouns ending in a consonant and **o**, add **es**.
   Ex: potato - potatoes
   Exceptions: photo - photos; piano - pianos

7) To most musical nouns ending in **o**, just add **s**.
   Ex: piano - pianos; solo - solos; soprano - sopranos

8) To most nouns ending in **f** or **fe**, add **s**.
   Ex: chief - chiefs; roof - roofs
   To some nouns ending in **f** or **fe**, change the **f** to **v** and add **es**.
   Ex: wife - wives; hoof - hooves

9) Some nouns have irregular plural forms.
   Ex: tooth - teeth; mouse - mice; appendix - appendices

10) Some nouns have the same form in both the singular and plural.
    Ex: moose - moose

11) Numbers, symbols, letters, and words discussed as a word usually form their plurals by adding an apostrophe **s**.
    Ex: 1990's; p's and q's

Write the plural form of the following nouns:

1) tomato
2) story
3) glass
4) man
5) sheep
6) floor
7) lunch
8) stereo
9) knife
10) goose
11) roof
12) glove
13) church
14) bush
15) deer
16) piano
17) life
18) ferry
19) hero
20) fox

2. a. Review the list of prepositions in Lesson 14. Put parentheses around all the prepositional phrases in the literature passage. Remember, in order for a word to be a preposition it must have an object. The object will always be a noun or pronoun.

b. The word *to* can be a preposition when it has an object, but in each place where *to* is used in this literature passage, it is followed by a verb. Underline each *to* and the verb following it. The verb following the word *to* is a kind of verbal called an infinitive. **Verbals** are words that are formed from verbs, but are used as other parts of speech. They are never used as verbs in a sentence, even though they can show action and be modified by adverbs.

Infinitives can act as adjectives, adverbs, or nouns, but most commonly act as nouns.
Ex: He has always wanted *to sing*.
(*To sing* is a noun acting as a direct object.)

This is the place *to be*.
(*To be* is an adjective modifying *place*.)

He ran in the race *to win*.
(*To win* is an adverb modifying *ran*.)

1.
e. 1) tomatoes
2) stories
3) glasses
4) men
5) sheep
6) floors
7) lunches
8) stereos
9) knives
10) geese
11) roofs
12) gloves
13) churches
14) bushes
15) deer
16) pianos
17) lives
18) ferries
19) heroes
20) foxes

2
a. of his circle
of flame
inside his circle
for him
with all four feet
in the coals
with terror
at the same time
in the snow

b. to get
to step
to meet
to drive
to cool

c. An **infinitive phrase** is a phrase with an infinitive and any modifiers or complements that accompany it. An infinitive phrase can act as a noun, adjective, or adverb.
Ex: To know me is to love me.
(*To know me* is the subject. *To love me* is the predicate nominative.)

Lindsey will give you the money to go to lunch.
(*To go to lunch* is an adjective modifying *money*.)

She ran to pick up the baby.
(*To pick up the baby* is an adverb modifying *ran*.)

d.
1) Jack Horner had <u>to sit</u> in the corner <u>to eat</u> his Christmas pie.
2) He was delighted <u>to put</u> in his thumb and pull out a plum.
3) He decided <u>to enjoy</u> his plum right then.
4) His mother was pleased <u>to see</u> him so well-behaved.
5) <u>To be</u> a good boy is always desirable.

d. Underline the infinitive phrases in each of these sentences:
1) Jack Horner had to sit in the corner to eat his Christmas pie.
2) He was delighted to put in his thumb and pull out a plum.
3) He decided to enjoy his plum right then.
4) His mother was pleased to see him so well-behaved.
5) To be a good boy is always desirable.

e. Two more facts to know about infinitives:
1) To check if an infinitive is acting as an adverb, insert the words *in order* before it. This will usually make sense. Ex: She ran *in order* to pick up the baby.

2) Sometimes the word *to* will be omitted from an infinitive. This is common after these verbs: *feel, see, dare, need, watch, help, make, let,* and *hear*.

f. to get (noun)
**   to step (noun)**
**   to meet (adverb)**
**   to drive (adverb)**
**   to cool (adverb)**

f. Write the infinitive phrases found in the literature passage. Indicate if they are nouns, adjectives, or adverbs.

g. to her cheeks - prepositional phrase; cheeks (object)

**   to buy - infinitive**

**   to buy - infinitive**

g. There are three phrases beginning with *to* in the literature passage in Lesson 3. Find them and indicate if they are prepositional phrases or infinitive phrases. If it is a prepositional phrase, name the object of the preposition.

3. a. Review verb tenses in Lesson 3. Underline all the action verbs in this week's literature passage. (Do not include the verbs acting as infinitives.)

   b. In what tense is this literature passage written - past, present, or future?

   c. Rewrite the literature passage in the present tense.
      Ex: Dawn comes, and daylight. The fire is burning low…

   d. Now rewrite the literature passage as if the action will take place tomorrow (future tense).
      Ex: Dawn will come, and daylight. The fire will burn low…

      What word did you have to use often as a helping verb?

   e. Write a sentence telling what you think might happen next in this story.

4. a. Make a list of the action verbs you underlined in **3a**. Write the infinitive, the present participle, past, and past participle form of each verb. Indicate whether the verb is regular (**R**) or irregular (**IR**).

   b. You have already underlined the verbs in the literature passage. Adverbs modify verbs, adjectives, and other adverbs. Ask the following adverb questions about each verb to find the adverbs: How? When? Where? To what extent or degree? Circle the adverbs.

3.
a. came, burning, run, attempted, surged, made, spring, strove, gave, stumbled, leaped, missed, landed, cried, scrambled

b. past tense

c. Dawn comes, and daylight. The fire is burning low. The fuel runs out, and there is need to get more. The man attempts to step out of his circle of flame, but the wolves surge to meet him. Burning brands make them spring back. In vain he strives to drive them back. As he gives up and stumbles inside his circle, a wolf leaps for him, misses and lands with all four feet in the coals. It cries out with terror, at the same time snarling, and scrambles back to cool its paws in the snow.

d. Dawn will come, and daylight. The fire will burn low. The fuel will run out, and there will be need to get more. The man will attempt to step out of his circle of flame, but the wolves will surge to meet him. Burning brands will make them spring back. In vain he will strive to drive them back. As he will give up and stumble inside his circle, a wolf

will leap for him, will
miss and land with all
four feet in the coals. It
will cry out with terror, at
the same time will
snarl, and scramble back
to cool its paws in the
snow.

will

e. Answers will vary.

4.
a. Answer is found at the
   end of this lesson.

b. low, out, out, back, back,
   up, out, back

c. *burning* modifies
   brands

   snarling modifies It

d. *pretending* things

f.
1) <u>Flying</u> was Orville and
   Wilbur's heart desire.
2) Many people had
   designed vehicles for
   <u>soaring</u> above the
   clouds.
3) The brothers tried
   <u>building</u> a glider.
4) <u>Praying</u> hard, they took
   off.
5) They were
   congratulated for <u>being</u>
   successful.

c. In **2b**, we learned that infinitives are a kind of verbal. Another kind of verbal is a participle. A **participle** is a verb form that is used as an adjective.
Ex: The *cheering* fans jumped to their feet.
The word *cheering* is formed from the verb *cheer* and acts as an adjective modifying the noun *fans*.

Ex: The pirates found the *hidden* treasure.
The word *hidden* is formed from the verb *hide* and acts as an adjective modifying the noun *treasure*.

Find two participles in the literature passage. What noun does it modify?

d. Find the participle in the literature passage in Lesson 4. What noun does it modify?

e. There is one other type of verbal - the gerund. A **gerund** is a verbal with an **-ing** ending that is used as a noun.
Ex: *Keeping* a journal is a good way to express your thoughts.

In the literature passage in Lesson 12, you read this phrase: "it could not be expected to have the power of smelling." *Of smelling* is a prepositional phrase, *of* being the preposition and *smelling* the noun acting as the object of the preposition. *Smelling* is a gerund here.

f. Since gerunds are nouns, use the possessive form of nouns and pronouns before a gerund.
Ex: (Incorrect) I was happy about Matt winning the race.
      (Correct) I was happy about *Matt's* winning the race.

      (Incorrect) It was hard to take him teasing me.
      (Correct) It was hard to take *his* teasing me.

Underline the gerunds in the following sentences:
1) Flying was Orville and Wilbur's dream.
2) Many people had designed vehicles for soaring above the clouds.
3) The brothers tried building a glider.
4) Praying hard, they took off.
5) They were congratulated for being successful.

5. a. Take a spelling test of the words you misspelled this week.

   b. Read the list of verbs you made in **4a**. It is a list of strong action verbs. They help convey the tension and excitement of this scene. Notice that although the infinitives are acting as nouns, they suggest action, too, making this truly an action packed scene.

      Using the sentence you wrote in **3e**, continue writing what you think might happen next. Continue to use strong verbs and infinitives.

   c. Choose skills from the *Review Activities* on the next page.

Answers:

4. a.

Infinitive	Present Participle	Past	Past Participle
come (IR)	coming	came	(have) come
burn (IR)	burning	burned	(have) burnt
run (IR)	running	ran	(have) run
attempt (R)	attempting	attempted	(have) attempted
surge (R)	surging	surged	(have) surged
make (IR)	making	made	(have) made
spring (IR)	springing	sprang, sprung	(have) sprung
strive (IR)	striving	strove	(have) striven
give (IR)	giving	gave	(have) given
stumble (R)	stumbling	stumbled	(have) stumbled
leap (IR)	leaping	leaped	(have) leapt
miss (R)	missing	missed	(have) missed
land (R)	landing	landed	(have) landed
cry (R)	crying	cried	(have) cried
scramble (R)	scrambling	scrambled	(have) scrambled

Review Activities

Choose skills your student needs to review.

1. *Plural Nouns*
Write the plural form of these nouns:

    a. girl
    b. dish
    c. butterfly
    d. key
    e. rodeo
    f. hero
    g. handkerchief
    h. loaf
    i. hoof

2. *Infinitive and Preposition*
Read the following literature passage from *White Fang*.
Underline the word *to* every time it is used. Above each *to*
indicate if it is used as in an infinitive (**I**) or in a prepositional
phrase (**PP**).

    The cub came upon it suddenly. It was his own fault. He
    had been careless. He had left the cave and run down to the
    stream to drink. It might have been that he took no notice
    because he was heavy with sleep. (He had been out all night
    on the meat trail, and had but just then awakened.) And his
    carelessness might have been due to the familiarity of the trail
    to the pool. He had traveled it often, and nothing had ever
    happened on it.

3. *Participles and Gerunds*
Are the underlined words in these sentences from *White Fang*
participles, gerunds, or verbs?

    a. He suppressed the whimper for fear that it might attract the
    attention of the <u>lurking</u> dangers.
    b. By the middle of the third day, he had been <u>running</u>
    continuously for thirty hours.
    c. The ropes of <u>varying</u> length prevented the dogs attacking
    from the rear those that ran in front of them.
    d. But a still greater <u>cunning</u> lurked in the recesses of the
    Indian mind.
    e. Thus, White Fang was kept in <u>training</u>.

1.
a. girls
b. dishes
c. butterflies
d. keys
e. rodeos
f. heroes
g. handkerchiefs
h. loaves
i. hooves

2.
to the stream
(prepositional phrase)

to drink (infinitive)

to the familiarity
(prepositional phrase)

to the pool
(prepositional phrase)

3.
a. participle
b. verb
c. participle
d. gerund
e. gerund

Pausing an instant, we made a bandage for my wounded finger, which was bleeding freely and ached severely, the bone being much bruised. Then we rode on, asking of our good horses all that was in them. The excitement of the fight and of our great resolve died away, and we rode in gloomy silence. Day broke clear and cold. We found a farmer just up, and made him give us sustenance for ourselves and our horses. I, feigning a toothache, muffled my face closely. Then ahead again, till Strelsau lay before us. It was eight o'clock or nearing nine, and the gates were open, as they always were save when the duke's caprice or intrigues shut them.

The Prisoner of Zenda by Anthony Hope

✎ **Teacher's Note:** As your student completes each lesson, choose skills from the *Review Activities* that he needs. The *Review Activities* follow each lesson.

1. a. Write the literature passage from dictation. Compare to the model and make corrections. Add any misspelled words to your *Personal Spelling List.*

   b. Take a spelling test of the next ten words from the *Commonly Misspelled Words List.* If you miss any words, add them to your *Personal Spelling List* and study them this week.

   c. Practice locating prepositional phrases by putting parentheses around them in the literature passage. What two words in the literature passage, acting as adverbs, can be prepositions when they have an object?

1.
c. for my wounded finger
   of our good horses
   of the fight
   of our great resolve
   in gloomy silence
   for ourselves and our horses
   before us

   We road <u>on</u>
   a farmer just <u>up</u>

2.

a. *resolve* - fixed purpose of mind

sustenance - that which supports life

feigning - making a false show

caprice - sudden change of mind

intrigues - plots to effect some purpose by secret artifices

b-d. pausing <u>an instant</u> (participle modifying *we*)

bleeding <u>freely</u>

asking <u>of our good horses</u> (participle modifying *we*)

being <u>much bruised</u> (participle modifying *bone*)

feigning <u>a toothache</u> (participle modifying *I*)

nearing <u>nine</u> (participle modifying *nine*)

---

2. a. Vocabulary Builder - resolve, sustenance, feigning, caprice, intrigues

   Write a dictionary sounding definition for each of these words using the context clues and your own knowledge. After looking them up in the *Glossary*, write a sentence using each word.

   b. The literature passage contains six words ending in the suffix **-ing**. Read the literature passage, and circle them.

   c. Each of these **-ing** words is followed by one or two words that complete the phrase. Underline these words.

   d. You should have the following phrases marked. Place a check (✔) beside the phrases that contain a participle. These are called **participial phrases**. Review Lesson 21 if you need help.

      pausing an instant
      bleeding freely
      asking of our good horses
      being much bruised
      feigning a toothache
      nearing nine

3. a. Review Lesson 20 about complements. Verbals, even though acting as nouns, adjectives, and adverbs, can have complements just as verbs do. The following chart summarizes the types of verbs and their complements.

Verb	—	Complement
transitive action verb	—	direct object, indirect object
intransitive action verb	—	none
linking verb	—	predicate adjective, predicate nominative

   b. The first participial phrase in the literature passage is *pausing an instant*. *Pausing* is a transitive action verb. To find out if a transitive verb has a direct object, ask the question *who* or *what*. If there is a noun or pronoun which answers the question, it is the direct object. *Pausing* what? *Instant* is the direct object.

c. Verbs and verbals can have indirect objects. An indirect object is a noun or pronoun that comes before the direct object and tells *to whom* or *for whom* the action of the verb is done.
Ex: Uncle Jim built the children a tree fort.

Uncle Jim built what? *Fort* is the direct object receiving the action *built*. *The children* tells *for whom* the fort was built. *Children* is the indirect object.

Hint
If the sentence does not have a direct object, it will not have an indirect object.

The same information that an indirect object gives can be given by a prepositional phrase. In that case, the noun or pronoun would be the object of the preposition not an indirect object.
Ex: Uncle Jim built a fort for the children.
For the children is a prepositional phrase. *Children* is the object of the preposition *for*.

d. Underline the direct object in each of the following sentences. If the sentence also has an indirect object, circle it.
1) The bedraggled princess banged the door with the knocker.
2) A servant opened the door.
3) She gave her a warm drink.
4) The princess climbed the ladder to the top of an unusually high bed.
5) She did not close her eyes all night.
6) In the morning, the princess found a pea under her mattress.

3.
d. 1) The bedraggled princess banged the **door** with the knocker.
2) A servant opened the **door.**
3) She gave (her) a warm **drink.**
4) The princess climbed the **ladder** to the top of an unusually high bed.
5) She did not close her **eyes** all night.
6) In the morning, the princess found a **pea** under her mattress.

3.
e.   1) made (action)
    2) was bleeding
       (action)
    3) ached (action)
    4) being (linking)
    5) rode (action)
    6) was (linking)
    7) died (action)
    8) rode (action)
    9) broke (action)
    10) found (action)
       farmer (direct
       object)
    11) made (action)
       him (direct object)
    12) give (action)
       us (indirect object)
       sustenance (direct
       object)
    13) muffled (action)
       face (direct object)
    14) lay (action)
    15) was (linking)
    16) were (linking)
    17) were (linking)
    18) shut (action)
       them (direct object)

e. Using this list of verbs found in this week's literature passage, decide if each verb is an action verb or a linking verb. If action, does it have an object? If so, write the direct object. If it has a direct object, is there an indirect object? If so write the indirect object.
    Ex: Terri wrote Mary a letter.
    wrote - action verb
    letter - direct object
    Mary - indirect object

    1) made
    2) was bleeding
    3) ached
    4) being
    5) rode
    6) was
    7) died
    8) rode
    9) broke
    10) found
    11) made
    12) give
    13) muffled
    14) lay
    15) was
    16) were
    17) were
    18) shut

4. a. Let's analyze the phrases containing the linking verbs you labeled in **3e**.
        that was in them
        it was eight o'clock or nearing nine
        gates were open
        as they always were

    1) that was in them
        That is the subject; *was* is the verb. What is *in them*? *In them* is a prepositional phrase acting as an adverb telling *where*.

    2) it was eight o'clock or nearing nine
        What is the subject of this sentence? The pronoun *it* is the subject and identified by two predicate nominatives connected by the conjunction *or*. This is an example of a compound predicate nominative.

    3) as they always were
        They is the subject and *were* the verb. *Always* is an adverb telling *to what extent*.

b. In Lesson 20 **4a,** you learned about predicate nominatives. Predicate nominatives are nouns or pronouns that identify or rename the subject. Linking verbs may also be followed by adjectives that tell about the subject.
Look at this phrase:

> *the gates were open*

What does *open* tell you about the subject *gates*? *Open* is an adjective telling what kind of gates, *open gates.*

c. Most adjectives and adverbs can indicate differing degrees such as *soft, softer*, or *softest.* By changing the form you can compare the degree of softness.

The **positive degree** is the base form of the adjective or adverb.
Ex: (adjective)   kind
      (adverb)   close

The **comparative degree** is used when comparing two things. Generally, **-er** is added to one or two-syllable modifiers. *More* is used with modifiers of three or more syllables. Two-syllable modifiers may use *more* if it is less awkward than the **-er** ending. Some words are acceptable either way.
Ex: (adjective) kinder
      (adverb)   closer
      (adjective) courteous, more courteous
      (adverb)   carefully, more carefully

Hint
Never use **-er** with *more.* Ex: more darker (This is incorrect.)

Hint
Adverbs ending in **-ly** usually use the word *more* in the comparative degree. Ex: more patiently

d. The **superlative degree** is used when comparing three or more of something. It is formed by adding **-est** or by using the word *most,* following the same general rules as using **-er** or *more* in the comparative degree.
Ex: (adjective) kindest, most courteous
(adverb) closest, most carefully

e. *Less* and *least* can also be used when comparing decreasing degrees of a quality. *Less, least, more,* and *most* all act as adverbs modifying the adjective or adverb compared.

f. Adjectives and adverbs whose comparative and superlative degrees are formed by adding **-er, -est,** or *more, most* are called **regular comparisons**. There is a small group of modifiers whose comparative and superlative degrees are formed differently. These are called **irregular comparisons**.

Positive	Comparative	Superlative
good	better	best
bad	worse	worst

g. Write the comparative and superlative degree of these modifiers found in this week's literature passage:
1) severely   5) clear
2) good   6) cold
3) great   7) closely
4) gloomy

h. Read the following Comparison Tips:

Comparison Tips

1) Do not make double comparisons.
Ex: This cake is more better. (incorrect)
This cake is better than that cake. (correct)
2) When comparing two things, use the comparative degree.
3) When comparing three or more things, use the superlative degree.
4) Make clear comparisons.
Ex: I like hamburgers more than Tim. (unclear)
I like hamburgers more than Tim likes hamburgers. (clear)

4.
g. 1) severely
more severely
most severely

2) good
better
best

3) great
greater
greatest

4) gloomy
gloomier
gloomiest

5) clear
clearer
clearest

6) cold
cold
colder

7) closely
more closely
most closely

i. Two pairs of adjectives and adverbs that are frequently
    confused are *good/well* and *bad/badly*. *Good* is <u>always</u> an
    adjective. *Good* should never be used as an adverb.
    Ex: (Incorrect) Michael Jordan plays basketball *good*.
          (Correct) Michael Jordan is a *good* basketball player.

Well can be used as an adjective meaning *healthy* but is
usually used as an adverb meaning *in a good or proper way*.
Ex: The pediatrician was glad to see a *well* child.
      (adjective)
      Eric plays piano *well*.
      (adverb)

Good / well is the positive form. The comparative and
superlative degrees for both words are the same: better, best.
Ex: John is a *good* basketball player. (positive adjective)
      Jill is a *better* basketball player than John.
      (comparative adjective)
      Of all the players, Chad is the *best* basketball player.
      (superlative adjective)

Ex: John plays basketball *well*. (positive adverb)
      Jill plays basketball *better* than John. (comparative
      adverb)
      Out of all the players, Chad plays *best*. (superlative
      adverb)

Bad is <u>always</u> an adjective. *Badly* is <u>always</u> an adverb.
Ex: (Incorrect) We felt *bad* when we lost the game.
      (Correct) We felt *badly* when we lost the game.

Bad / badly is the positive form. The comparative and
superlative degrees for both words are the same: worse,
worst.

5. a. Take a spelling test of the words you misspelled this week.

   b. There are three pairs of verbs which are sometimes confusing because they look similar and their meanings are similar. One of these pairs is *lay / lie*.

   The sentence in our literature passage reads:

   > *Then ahead again, till Strelsau* lay *before us.*

   The word *lay* in the literature passage uses a verb form of *lie*. *Lie* means *to rest* or *to recline* or *to remain in a certain state or position*. *Lie* is an intransitive verb. It does not take an object.
   Ex: Our cat *lies* in the sun all day.

   Lay means *to put something* or *to place something*. *Lay* is a transitive verb needing an object.
   Ex: The nurse *has laid* the baby down.

   Look at the principal parts of *lie* and *lay*.

Infinitive	Present Participle	Past	Past Participle
lie	(be) lying	lay	(have) lain
lay	(be) laying	laid	(have) laid

   The confusion usually occurs when using a form of *lay* when a form of *lie* is correct. Here are a couple of guidelines to help you decide which verb you should use:
   1) Does the verb in the sentence take an object? If so, you need to use a form of *lay*.
   2) If you can replace the verb with *put* and it makes sense, use a form of *lay*.

c. Fill in the blanks in the following sentences with a form of *lie* or *lay*.
1) The book was (*lying, laying*) open on the table.
2) She (*lay, laid*) the money on the counter.
3) The children (*lay, laid*) in the shade after the picnic.
4) If you become tired, (*lie, lay*) down and rest.
5) Mother (*laid, lay*) the children's pajamas out.
6) After having (*lain, laid*) down for a nap, he felt better.
7) Be careful not to (*lie, lay*) the blame on the wrong person.
8) Dad is (*lying, laying*) tiles in the bathroom.

d. Another pair of verbs that can be confusing is *rise* and *raise*. *Rise* means *to go to a higher position*. *Rise* is an intransitive verb. It does not take an object.
Ex   Everyone will *rise* when the bride appears.

Raise means *to lift something* or *to increase something*. *Raise* is a transitive verb needing an object.
Ex: Will you *raise* the flag?

Look at the principle parts of *rise* and *raise*:

Infinitive	Present Participle	Past	Past Participle
rise	(be) rising	rose	(have) risen
raise	(be) raising	raised	(have) raised

Try replacing the verb *rise* or *raise* with *lift* in the sentence. If it makes sense, use a form of *raise*.

e. Fill in the blanks in these sentences with a form of the verbs *rise* or *raise*.
1) When the cannon sounded, the American flag was (*risen, raised*).
2) Is the bread (*rising, raising*) properly?
3) The guest speaker (*raised, rose*) from his seat.
4) Our family has (*raised, rose*) corn for generations.
5) The soprano's voice should (*rise, raise*) at the end of the song.
6) The cost of living has (*risen, raised*) this year.
7) We will be (*rising, raising*) before dawn to go fishing.
8) Then an important question was (*raised, risen*).

5.
c. 1) The book was *lying* open on the table.
2) She *laid* the money on the counter.
3) The children *lay* in the shade after the picnic.
4) If you become tired, *lie* down and rest.
5) Mother *laid* the children's pajamas out.
6) After having *lain* down for a nap, he felt better.
7) Be careful not to *lay* the blame on the wrong person.
8) Dad is *laying* tiles in the bathroom.

e.
1) When the cannon sounded, the American flag was *raised*.
2) Is the bread *rising* properly?
3) The guest speaker *rose* from his seat.
4) Our family has *raised* corn for generations.
5) The soprano's voice should *rise* at the end of the song.
6) The cost of living has has *risen* this year.
7) We will be *rising* before dawn to go fishing.
8) Then an important question was *raised*.

f. The final set of confusing verbs is *sit* and *sat*. *Sit* means *to assume an upright sitting position*. *Sit* is an intransitive verb and does not take an object.
Ex: She always *sits* there.

Set means *to place something*. *Set* is transitive and takes an object.
Ex: The children *set* their books on the bench.

Look at the principal parts of *sit* and *set*:

Infinitive	Present Participle	Past	Past Participle
sit	(be) sitting	sat	(have) sat
set	(be) setting	set	(have) set

g. Fill in the following blanks in these sentences with a form of the verbs *sit* or *set*.
1) The children could not (*sit, set*) still for long.
2) We (*sat, set*) the pie out to cool.
3) The teacher had been (*sitting, setting*) down too long.
4) Please (*set, sit*) down your packages.
5) We tried (*sitting, setting*) still.
6) Dad always (*sits, sets*) his keys on the mantle.
7) After (*sitting, setting*) the timer, Mom put the cookies in the oven.
8) I felt I had been (*sitting, setting*) there for hours.

h. Write the comparative and superlative form of these modifiers taken from the literature passage used in Lesson 6.
1) broad   8) exceedingly
2) few   9) bright
3) common   10) dark
4) large   11) confused
5) raggedly   12) white
6) long   13) naturally
7) hollow   14) yellow

i. Choose skills from the *Review Activities* on the next page.

5.
g. 1) The children could not *sit* still for long.
2) We *set* the pie out to cool.
3) The teacher had been *sitting* down too long.
4) Please *set* down your packages.
5) We tried *sitting* still.
6) Dad always *sets* his keys on the mantle.
7) After *setting* the timer, Mom put the cookies in the oven.
8) I felt I had been *sitting* there for hours.

h. 1) broad, broader, broadest
2) few, fewer, fewest
3) common, commoner, commonest (could be more common and most common)
4) large, larger, largest
5) raggedly, more raggedly, most raggedly
6) long, longer, longest
7) hollow, more hollow, most hollow
8) exceedingly, more exceedingly, most exceedingly
9) bright, brighter, brightest
10) dark, darker, darkest
11) confused, more confused, most confused
12) white, whiter, whitest
13) naturally, more naturally, most naturally
14) yellow, yellower, yellowest

Review Activities

Choose skills your student needs to review.

1. *Prepositional Phrase*
   Copy this paragraph from *The Prisoner of Zenda*. Put parentheses around the prepositional phrases.

   We went in and reached the dressing-room. Flinging open the door, we saw Fritz von Tarlenheim stretched, fully dressed, on the sofa. He seemed to have been sleeping, but our entry woke him. He leapt to his feet, gave one glance at me, and with a joyful cry, threw himself on his knees before me.

2. *Participial Phrase and Direct Object*
   Underline the participial phrases. If the participial phrase has a direct object, circle it.

3. *Direct and Indirect Object*
   Underline the verb in each of these sentences. Circle the direct object, and draw a box around the indirect object.

   a. Androcles ran away from his master.
   b. He lived in a cave with a friendly lion.
   c. The lion brought him food.
   d. Androcles was captured.
   e. He was taken to Rome.
   f. He faced a hungry lion in the Coliseum.
   g. He hugged his old friend.
   h. The crowd cheered.

4. *Comparative and Superlative Degrees*
   Write the comparative and superlative degree of these modifiers:

   a. tall
   b. helpful
   c. far
   d. popular
   e. shy
   f. slow
   g. sternly
   h. gently

---

1. on the sofa
   to his feet
   at me
   with a joyful cry
   on his knees
   before me

2. **Flinging open the door**
   (door - direct object)
   fully dressed

3.
   a. ran (verb)
   b. lived (verb)
   c. brought (verb)
      food (direct object)
      him (indirect object)
   d. was captured (verb)
   e. was taken (verb)
   f. faced (verb)
      lion (direct object)
   g. hugged (verb)
      friend (direct object)
   h. cheered (verb)

4.
   a. tall, taller, tallest
   b. helpful, more helpful, most helpful
   c. far, farther, farthest
   d. popular, more popular, most popular
   e. shy, shyer, shyest
   f. slow, slower, slowest
   g. sternly, more sternly, most sternly
   h. gently, more gently, most gently

5.

  a. lying

  b. rising

  c. set

  d. good

  e. rose

  f. bad

  g. lay

  h. sat

  i. well

  j. badly

5. *Correct Word Usage*

Fill in the blank with the correct word:

a. His socks were (*lying, laying*) on the bed.
b. Gina watched the smoke (*raising, rising*).
c. Please don't (*sit, set*) your glass on this table.
d. Jenny enjoyed reading the (*well, good*) book.
e. After the superb performance, the audience (*rose, raised*) as one, wildly applauding.
f. Sara felt (*bad, badly*) about what she said.
g. She could not (*lay, lie*) the book down.
h. David (*sat, set*) in the seat by the window.
i. Sam could write (*well, good*).
j. Andrew played his violin (*bad, badly*) at the audition.

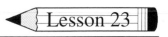

So he sent and brought him in. Now he was ruddy, with beautiful eyes and a handsome appearance. And the Lord said, "Arise, anoint him for this is he." Then Samuel took the horn of oil and anointed him in the midst of his brothers; and the Spirit of the Lord came mightily upon David from that day forward. And Samuel arose and went to Ramah.

I Samuel 16:12, 13 (NASB)

✎ **Teacher's Note:**
Lessons 23 and 24 use the same literature passage. As your student completes the lessons, choose skills from the *Review Activities* that he needs. The *Review Activities* follow Lesson 24.

1. a. Do you remember when to use quotation marks? Review by looking back at Lesson 11. There is a direct quote in this literature passage. Listen as your teacher reads the passage. Did you hear the direct quote? It was the Lord saying, "Arise, anoint him, for this is he."

   b. Write the literature passage from dictation. Compare with the model and make corrections. Add any misspelled words to your *Personal Spelling List*.

   c. Take a spelling test of the next ten words from the *Commonly Misspelled Words List*. Add any words you misspell to your *Personal Spelling List* to be studied this week.

   d. Vocabulary Builder - ruddy, anoint

   Write a dictionary sounding definition for each word using the context clues and your own knowledge. Look up the words in the *Glossary*, and then write a sentence using each one.

2. a. There are seven personal pronouns in the literature passage. Circle them. Look back at Lesson 2 to review pronouns if needed.

   b. You will remember that pronouns can be plural or singular. They can also show person (1st, 2nd, 3rd) and possession. Look at the pronouns you circled in **2a**. Find the possessive pronoun. What is it possessing?

1.
d. *ruddy* - the color of human skin in high health
anoint - to consecrate by the use of oil

2
a. he, him, he, him, he, him, his

b. his <u>brothers</u>

2.

c. he (sent)
  he (was)

  anoint him (direct object)
  anointed him (direct object)

d. Now he was ruddy (predicate adjective)
  this is he (predicate nominative)

  A subjective pronoun is used because it renames the subject.

e.
1) him
2) she
3) He, me
4) they
5) she, I
6) me, we

f. this - singular
  these - plural

3.
a. Arise, anoint him for this is he.

---

c. Pronouns can also act as subjects or objects in a sentence. Find the two pronouns circled which act as subjects of the sentence. Pronouns that act as subjects are called **subjective pronouns**. Pronouns which act as objects are called **objective pronouns**. Find an example of an objective pronoun in the first sentence.

Him is the direct object of the verb *brought*. What kinds of objects are the other two objective pronouns in the literature passage?

d. Find an example of a predicate nominative and a predicate adjective in the literature passage. Refer to Lesson 20, **4a-b** if you need a review. Is an objective or subjective pronoun used when acting as a predicate nominative? Why?

e. Choose the correct objective or subjective pronoun to complete the following sentences:
1) Is that present for (*he, him*)?
2) Shelly and (*she, her*) are taking it to the party.
3) (*He, Him*) also invited Jason and (*I, me*).
4) You and (*they, them*) should go together.
5) Either (*she, her*) or (*I, me*) will pick you up.
6) Mother asked Jane and (*I, me*) if (*we, us*) had a good time.

f. A demonstrative pronoun points out a particular person or thing. Find the demonstrative pronoun in the literature passage. It is in the singular form. What would be the plural form?

3. a. Find the imperative sentence in the literature passage. Refer to Lesson 20, **2b** if you need a review.

b. The word *conjunction* comes from the Latin words *con* meaning together and *jungere* meaning *to join*. Conjunctions are little words that connect other words or groups of words. Refer to Lesson 4, **3d** about conjunctions if you need a review.

Coordinating conjunctions link the same kinds of words or sentence parts together. *And*, *but*, and *or* are the most commonly used coordinating conjunctions. Underline the word *and* every time it is used in the literature passage. Indicate what kind of words or groups of words are joined together by each *and*.

The word *for* may also be a coordinating conjunction, used to join two independent clauses. Underline the conjunction *for* in the literature passage.

c. Fill in this pronoun chart.

Subjective	Objective	Possessive
you		
it		
I		
he		
she		
we		
they		

4. a. Look at the literature passage. With a red pencil, box in the adverbs. Refer to Lesson 10, **3c-e** if you need a review.

   b. With a blue pencil, box in the two adjectives found in the literature passage. (Do not box in the articles.) Refer to Lesson 6 if you need a review.

3.
b. sent and brought (compound verb)

beautiful and a handsome appearance (compound object of preposition)

took and anointed (compound verb)

arose and went (compound verb)

The other three <u>ands</u> connect sentences. (compound sentences)

✎ Teacher's Note: Generally, sentences are not begun with a conjunction, but authors can take liberties.

c. | Objective | Possessive |
|---|---|
| you | your, yours |
| it | its |
| me | my, mine |
| him | his |
| her | her, hers |
| us | our, ours |
| them | their, theirs |

4.
a. in, Now, Then, mightily, forward
b. beautiful
    handsome

4.

d. and e.

1) with beautiful eyes and a handsome appearance (adjective modifying *he*)

2) of oil (adjective modifying *horn*)

3) in the midst (adverb modifying *anoint*)

4) of his brothers (adverb modifying prepositional phrase *in the midst*)

5) of the Lord (adjective modifying *Spirit*)

6) upon David (adverb modifying *came*)

7) from that day (adverb modifying *came*)

8) to Ramah (adverb modifying *went*)

5.

b. 1) in silence (adverb)
2) for a time (adverb)
3) of Colosse (adjective)
4) with marigolds and daisies (adverb)
5) of half-grown lambs (adjective)
6) of the dams (adjective)
7) of the stream (adjective)
8) as a little boy (adjective)
9) for these sights and sounds (adverb)
10) in Rome (adverb)
11) with dread and foreboding (adverb)

c. Prepositional phrases can act as either adjectives or adverbs. When a prepositional phrase is modifying a noun or pronoun it is acting as an adjective. When a prepositional phrase is modifying a verb, adjective, or adverb it acts as an adverb. When a prepositional phrase follows another prepositional phrase, it may be modifying that prepositional phrase.

Ex: adjective prepositional phrase: The lemonade *in the glass* had become watery.

adverb prepositional phrase: The moon rose *over the bay*.

prepositional phrase modifying another prepositional phrase: The basket of flowers on the table is beautiful.

d. List all the prepositional phrases found in the literature passage.

e. Using the list of the prepositional phrases, indicate if they are acting as an adjective (**Adj**) or an adverb (**Adv**), and write the words they modify.

5. a. Take a spelling test of the words you misspelled this week.

b. Find the prepositional phrases in the literature passage in Lesson 5. Write the prepositional phrases and indicate if they are adjective (**Adj**) or adverb (**Adv**) phrases.

c. Today you will begin preparing for your writing assignment for next week. The Bible contains long biographies of important historical characters. This week's literature passage tells something of the life of David.

Choose one Old Testament character, such as David, Abraham, or Joseph. Using a concordance, find the passages that tell about the character. Read the passages, asking the question: "Why is this person important?"

d. *Review Activities* for Lesson 23 are coupled with Lesson 24. See page 141.

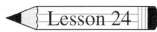

1. Take a spelling test of the next ten words from the *Commonly Misspelled Words List*. Add any words you misspell to your *Personal Spelling List* to be studied this week.

2. Read the chapters again about the biblical character you chose last week. As you read this time, use a pencil and paper to record important facts and events that occurred in his or her life. It would be helpful to keep things in chronological order. Most biographies begin at the beginning of someone's life, but another technique is to start at a later point and then flashback to fill in the details of earlier life. We discussed flashbacks in Lesson 16, **3c**.

3. After you have read the material and made notes of important facts and events, divide the information into an **outline**. This will help you organize your final paper. For example, if you were writing about Moses, your outline might be:

   I.   Moses' life as a child
   II. Moses' life in Pharaoh's household
   III. Moses' life in Moab
   IV. Moses' life back in Egypt
   V.   Moses' life in the wilderness

   Place facts and events under each main heading. You now have your information organized in a natural flow. Look at the example below.

   > I. Moses' life as a child
   >
   >   A. Event
   >   1. Fact
   >   2. Fact
   >
   >   B. Event
   >   1. Fact
   >   2. Fact
   >
   > II. Moses' life in Pharaoh's household, etc.

4. On a separate piece of paper, begin writing. Use adjectives and adverbs wisely. Choose strong verbs and specific nouns. After writing your biography, put it aside until tomorrow. Distancing yourself will give you a fresher look at what you have written.

5. a. Read what you wrote yesterday. Is the story clearly told? If you are satisfied with the flow of the story and you have included all important facts and events, look at the smaller parts of the story. Does each paragraph contain related ideas? Is your sentence structure varied in length? Read the paper aloud. How does it sound? Now is the time to check mechanics: spelling, capitalization, and punctuation.

    When you are finished, make a neat final copy of your biography. If you have time, you might like to include appropriate illustrations, maps, etc.

    b. Take a spelling test of the words you misspelled this week.

    c. Choose skills from the *Review Activities* on the next page.

Review Activities

Choose skills your student needs to review.

1. *Pronouns*
   Choose the correct pronoun:

   a. (*Who*, *Whom*) are you looking for?
   b. The movie scared Jackie and (*I*, *me*).
   c. (*You*, *Your*) snoring kept me awake.
   d. Is that cake for (*me*, *I*) and (*him*, *he*)?
   e. You and (*her*, *she*) are invited.

2. *Predicate Adjective and Predicate Nominative*
   Is the underlined word in each sentence a predicate adjective or a predicate nominative?

   a. The emperor was <u>unhappy</u>.
   b. He was poorly <u>dressed</u>.
   c. His tailors were <u>crooks</u>.
   d. His advisors were <u>afraid</u>.
   e. The emperor was a <u>fool</u>.
   f. The little boy was <u>wise</u>.
   g. The emperor was <u>embarrassed</u>.

3. *Prepositional Phrases*
   Copy the following paragraph and put parentheses around the prepositional phrases.

   Once a man of humble means had a donkey that had served him faithfully for many long years. The donkey's strength was gone and it was now unfit for work. So his master began to consider how much he could get for the donkey's skin. The beast, in a state of alarm, ran away along the road to Bremen.

4. Are the prepositional phrases adjectives or adverbs?

1.
a. Whom
b. me
c. Your
d. me, him
e. she

2.
a. predicate adjective
b. predicate adjective
c. predicate nominative
d. predicate adjective
e. predicate nominative
f. predicate adjective
g. predicate adjective

3. and 4.
   of humble means - adjective

   for many long years - adverb

   for work - adjective

   for the donkey's skin - adverb

   in a state - adjective

   of alarm - adverb

   along the road - adverb

   to Bremen - adverb

Teacher's Note: As your student completes each lesson, choose skills from the *Review Activities* that he needs. The *Review Activities* follow each lesson.

Once we see the Bible's realism, we can understand why the Reformation produced a democracy of checks and balances. A Christian does not trust even himself with unlimited power. Calvin pointed out that because men are sinners it is better to be governed by the many rather than the few or a single man. Every Christian organization and every state built on the Reformation mentality is built to allow men freedom under God but not unlimited freedom. Unlimited freedom will not work in a lost world; some structure and form are necessary.

No Little People by Francis A. Schaeffer
(Used by permission, Edith Schaeffer)

1. a. Write the literature paragraph from dictation and then compare with the model. Correct any errors and add any misspelled words to your *Personal Spelling List*.

   b. Take a review spelling test of any words your teacher chooses from your *Personal Spelling List*. Add any words you misspelled from the dictation to your *Personal Spelling List* and study the list during this week.

   c. Is this literature passage an example of fiction or nonfiction writing?

   d. The literature passage is taken from a sermon by Dr. Francis A. Schaeffer. Discuss the passage with your teacher. If you are not sure what the Reformation was or what a democracy of checks and balances is, look them up in the encyclopedia.

2.
a. *realism* - the tendency to view things how they really are
democracy - government by the people
mentality - mental capacity

2. a. Vocabulary Builder - realism, democracy, mentality

   Write a dictionary sounding definition for these three words using any context clues or personal knowledge you may have. After looking them up in the *Glossary*, write a sentence using each word.

   b. In Lesson 4, you learned that sentence length provides a kind of rhythm for writing. Short sentences are forceful, while longer sentences create a smoother flow of thoughts. Too many short sentences can be boring for the reader.

Ex: The little old lady made a gingerbread man. She put
    him in the oven to bake. She opened the oven door.
    The gingerbread man winked at her.

Writing like this sounds as if it came out of a first grade
primer. Learning to combine and connect sentences will
make your writing more interesting. The easiest way to
combine two sentences is to connect them with a
coordinating conjunction.

The sample sentences above could be written:
    The little old lady made a gingerbread man and put him
    in the oven to bake. She opened the oven door and the
    gingerbread man winked at her.

Coordinating Conjunctions
and   but   nor   or   for

Two complete sentences have been combined by
connecting them with the conjunction *and*. In order for this
to work, the two sentences must relate. (Refer to Lesson
4, **3d-4e** if you need a review.) The conjunctions that you
have learned about, such as *and*, *but*, and *or* are called
coordinating conjunctions. Using coordinating
conjunctions may be the easiest way to combine sentences,
but it is not always the best way. A second method of
sentence combination is by making one of the sentences
dependent upon the other. This is accomplished by using a
subordinating conjunction.

Commonly Used Subordinating Conjunctions
since   although   when   because

A subordinating conjunction added to a complete
sentence makes it a dependent clause, thereby, an
incomplete statement, unable to stand alone. A
subordinating conjunction can appear at the beginning of a
sentence or within the body of the sentence.

Ex: She opened the oven door. (This is a complete sentence.)

When she opened the oven door. (This is a dependent clause; thereby, an incomplete sentence.)

When she opened the oven door, the gingerbread man winked at her. (This is a complete sentence.)

A **clause** is a group of words containing a subject and predicate. A clause may be dependent or independent.

A comma usually separates the two clauses if the sentence begins with a dependent clause.

Ex: *When* she opened the oven door, the gingerbread man winked at her.

A comma is usually omitted if the sentence begins with an independent clause.

Ex: She opened the oven door *because* the gingerbread man was done.

Practice combining the following sentences. First, connect them with a coordinating conjunction and then rewrite the sentences using a subordinate conjunction.

1) The little old lady mixed up the gingerbread.
The little old lady formed a gingerbread man.

2) The gingerbread man would not stop running.
The little old man ran after the gingerbread man.

3) The water rose higher.
The gingerbread man moved from the fox's back to his head.

4) The little old lady and the little old man ran on.
The little old lady and the little old man were getting tired.

c. The last sentence in the literature passage is an example of another way to connect sentences. Sentences may be joined together with punctuation. In this case a semicolon (;) is used. **Colons** (:) also can be used to emphasize an important idea.

2.

b. Possible answer:

1) The little old lady mixed up the gingerbread and formed a gingerbread man.

When the little old lady had mixed up the gingerbread, she formed a gingerbread man.

2) The gingerbread man would not stop so the little old man ran after him.

Since the gingerbread man would not stop, the little old man ran after him.

3) The water rose higher and the gingerbread man moved from the fox's back to his head.

When the water rose higher, the gingerbread man moved from the fox's back to his head.

4) The little old lady and the little old man ran on but they were getting tired.

Although the little old lady and the little old man ran on, they were getting tired.

Ex: As they watched the fox gulp down the gingerbread man, no one felt sad for one important reason: gingerbread men are made to be eaten.

These methods are effective, but should be used sparingly.

d. Finally, here are three more methods used to combine clauses:
1) Sometimes you can combine clauses by making a series of the ideas.
   Ex: The gingerbread man jumped out of the oven, ran out of the kitchen door, and was chased through the garden by the little old man.

2) A relative pronoun may be used to introduce a subordinate clause.
   Ex: The little old man, *who* was working in his garden, was very surprised to see the gingerbread man running by.

3) Using a participial phrase (Lesson 22) is another excellent way to combine clauses.
   Ex: The gingerbread man ran down the road, *laughing* at the little old lady and the little old man.

e. Practice these methods of combination by rewriting the following sentences using the suggested method:
1) Using a series
   The gingerbread man jumped out of the oven.
   The gingerbread man ran down the road.
   The gingerbread man stopped to rest under a tree.

2) Using a relative pronoun
   The gingerbread man's behavior was unexpected.
   The gingerbread man quickly out ran the little old lady and the little old man.

3) Using a participial phrase
   The gingerbread man crossed the river.
   The gingerbread man left the little old lady and the little old man behind.

2.
e. 1) The gingerbread man jumped out of the oven, ran down the road, and stopped to rest under a tree.
2) The gingerbread man, whose behavior was unexpected, quickly out ran the little old lady and the little old man.
3) The gingerbread man crossed the river, leaving the little old lady and the little old man behind.

3.

a. In this article, the topic sentence is the first sentence of each paragraph.

3. a. One of the fundamentals of good study habits is the ability to take clear notes. Today you will practice **note taking** using printed material.

The following article was taken from an encyclopedia. It is an informational article about pencils. The first paragraph is the **introductory paragraph**, which introduces the topic. The first three paragraphs have clear **topic sentences** with **supporting sentences**. Underline the topic sentences in these paragraphs. The final paragraph is a **concluding paragraph** which includes information about the two final steps in the pencil making process.

Lead pencils really contain no lead. The marking material is a mixture of the mineral graphite and fine clay combined with certain chemicals and wax. When graphite was first used in pencils, people thought it contained lead. Therefore, they called it *lead* or *black lead*.

People still call the graphite mixture *lead* and the pencils *lead pencils.*

The amount of clay that pencil makers mix with graphite depends on how hard they wish to make the lead. The less clay they use, the softer and blacker the lead will be. To make lead, workers blend the clay and graphite with water in a high-speed mixer. This mixture is placed in a machine and squeezed out of a narrow opening as one long black string of lead. The lead is cut into pieces about 7 1/4 inches (18.4 centimeters) long. The pieces are then hardened in firing ovens. Finally, the pieces of lead are treated with a wax so they will write smoothly.

The wood cases for most pencils are made of incense cedar. This wood has a soft, straight *grain* (pattern) that permits easy sharpening without splitting.

<u>The World Book Encyclopedia</u> (1982), Volume 15, page 209.

Write, in your own words, a sentence that explains the topic of each paragraph. Or, if you like, write a question that would be answered by the information in the paragraph.

Ex: Most pencils have a wooden case and a black writing core.
OR What are cased pencils made of?

Next, make a list of brief facts stated in the supporting sentences of each paragraph, listing them under the paraphrased topic sentence or question you formulated. This is an informal way of taking notes about an informational article. You have actually made a rough outline of the article.

A more formal way of outlining is called the **topic outline**, a summary of topics using Roman numerals (I, II, III) and a summary of subtopics capital letters (A,B,C); and when necessary, Arabic numerals (1, 2, 3) and lower case letters (a, b, c) in that order. Periods are used after the numbers and letters. You may add a title to your outline. Look at the sample below.

```
                        Title

  I.  Main Topic
      A.  Subtopic
          1.  Subheading
              a.  Detail or example
              b.  Detail or example
          2.  Subheading
              a.  Detail or example
              b.  Detail or example
  II. Main Topic
      A.  Subtopic
          1.  Subheading
              a.  Detail or example
              b.  Detail or example
      B.  Subtopic
          1.  Subheading
              a.  Detail or example
              b.  Detail or example
              c.  Detail or example
          2.  Subheading
              a.  Detail or example
              b.  Detail or example
```

In an article or single chapter of a reference book, the Roman numerals (I, II, III) correspond to main topics. Capital letters (A, B, C) correspond to blocks of paragraphs. Arabic numbers (1, 2, 3) correspond to subheadings or paragraphs. Lower case letters (a, b, c) correspond to key sentences.

b. Write a topic outline of the pencil article.

3.
b. Possible answer:
   I. Lead pencils
      A. Contain no lead
         I. graphite
         2. fine clay
      B. Called lead pencils
   II. Hardness
   III. Making the lead
      A. mixture
      B. formation
   IV. Incense cedar

✎ Teacher's Note: Your student's outline may vary slightly.

c. Answers will vary.

4.
b. Answer is found at the end of this lesson.

5.
d. Possible answer:

    A parade came to our town to advertise the coming of the circus. The parade, which had clowns and jugglers, was led by a marching band. Being so exciting and colorful, it made everyone want to go to the circus.

c. Choose another short article in an encyclopedia or magazine to outline. Write an informal outline and a topic outline.

4. a. When listening to a lecture, you will find that you will be able to remember what was said more easily if you have cultivated the habit of listening with a pen in your hand. Taking notes while listening to a speaker takes a bit more concentration than taking notes about a printed article. Discuss the *Note Taking Tips*, found at the end of this lesson, with your teacher. Can you think of any other suggestions?

   b. Listen to your teacher as she reads the sermon, *Without Money and Without Price*, on the next page. Do not read it beforehand. It is a condensed version of a sermon given by Charles Spurgeon (1834-1892). Using the *Note Taking Tips* at the end of this lesson, take notes. When you are through, look over your notes. How did you do? What are the main points of the sermon? Write an outline of the sermon.

5. a. Take a spelling test of the words you misspelled this week.

   b. Practice your note taking skills by outlining a short chapter or article in your history or science book.

   c. If you have access to a taped sermon or speech, practice taking notes while listening to it. If not, practice your note taking while listening to a sermon at church or listen to a lecture or sermon given over the radio. This takes some work. Don't give up. With practice you will improve.

   d. Write a paragraph using the following information. Practice the suggested methods of combining sentences given to you in this lesson.

> There was a parade in our town.
> The parade came to advertise the circus.
> The parade had clowns and jugglers.
> The parade was led by a marching band.
> The parade was exciting.
> The parade was very colorful.
> The parade caused everyone in town to want to go to the circus.

e. Choose skills from the *Review Activities* which follow
    this lesson.

Without Money and Without Price

The gifts of God's grace are absolutely free in the most
unrestricted sense of that term. Nothing good, whatsoever is
brought by man, or is expected from man, by way of
recommendation to mercy; but everything is given gratis, and
is received by us "without money and without price." Upon
that one thought I shall dwell, hoping that the Spirit of God
will make it plain to your minds.

First, I shall notice the surprising nature of this fact, for it
is very surprising to mankind to hear that salvation is "without
money and without price." It is so surprising to them that the
plainest terms cannot make them understand it. They cannot
be brought to accept it as literally true that they are to have
everything for nothing. Now why is it that man does not see
this? Why is it that when he does see it he is surprised? I think
it is, first, because of man's relation to God, and his wrong
judgment of Him. Man thinks that God is a hard master.
When the Holy Spirit convinces men of sin they still retain
hard thoughts of God, and fear that he cannot be so gracious as
to blot out their sins. Little do they know that heart of love
which throbs in Jehovah's bosom.

No doubt, also, the condition of man under the fall makes it
more difficult for him to comprehend that the gifts of God are
"without money and without price," for he is doomed to toil
for almost everything he needs. He reads the words "without
money and without price" and thinks there must be something
written between the lines to modify the sense, for there must be
something to do or to feel before a sinner can receive the gifts
of grace.

Again, man recollects the general rule of men toward each
other, for in this world what is to be had for nothing except
that which is worth nothing? Nothing for nothing is the
general system. Dealing with our fellow-men, we must
naturally expect, even according to the golden rule, that we
should give them an equivalent for what we receive. And so
"without money and without price" is quite a novelty, and man
is astonished at it and cannot believe it to be true.

Another matter helps man into this difficult, namely, his
natural pride. He does not like to be a pauper before God.
Pride is woven into man's nature. We do not like to be saved

by charity, and so have no corner in which to sit and boast. You insult a moral man if you tell him that he must be saved in the same way as a thief or murderer, yet this is not more than the truth.

Thus I have spoken upon the surprising nature of this fact, but I want to add that, though I have thus shown grounds for our surprise, yet if men would think a little they might not be quite so unbelievingly amazed as they are; for after all, the best blessings we have come to us freely. What price have you paid for your lives? What price do you pay for the air you breathe? Life and air and light come to us "without money and without price." The senses are freely bestowed on us by God, and so is the sleep which rests them. We ought not, therefore, to be so surprised, after all, that the gifts of his grace are free.

In the second place, dear friends, I want to show you the necessity of the fact mentioned in our text. There was a necessity that the gifts of the gospel should be "without money and without price." A threefold necessity.

First, from the character of the donor. It is God that gives. Oh, sirs, would you have him sell his pardons? The King of Kings, would you have him vend forgiveness to the sons of men at so much per head? Would you have him sell his Holy Spirit, and would you come like Simon Magus and offer money unto him for it? Talk not so exceeding proudly. Salvation must be given without price, since it is God that gives.

Again, it must be for nothing, because of the value of the boon. As one has well said, "it is without price because it is priceless." The gospel is so precious a thing that if it is to be bought the whole world could not pay for it, and therefore if bought at all it must needs be without money and without price. It cost the Lord Jesus his blood, what have you to offer?

And there is another reason arising from the extremity of human destitution. The blessings of grace must be given "without money and without price," for we have no money or price to bring. Is not that good reasoning that God must give eternal life for nothing, because you have nothing which you could offer as a price? If you are to have eternal life, no terms but those of grace will meet your case.

My third point is this, the salutary influence of this fact. If it be "without money and without price," what then? Well, first, that enables us to preach the gospel to every creature. If we had to look for some price in the hand of the creature, or some fitness in the mind of the creature, or some excellence in the life of the creature we could not preach mercy to every creature, we should have to preach it to prepared creatures, and then that preparation would be the money and the price. The fact that the mercy of God is "without money and without price" enables us to preach it to every man, woman, and child of woman born.

Now, note secondly, that this fact has the salutary effect of excluding all pride. If it be "without money and without price," you rich people have not a halfpennyworth of advantage above the poorest of the poor in this matter. So that the pride of wealth is utterly abolished by the gospel; and so is the pride of merit. You have been so good and so charitable, and you are so excellent, and so religious, and so everything that you ought to be, and you fancy that there must be some private entrance, some reserved door for persons of your quality; but, sirs, the gate is so strait that you must rub shoulders with thieves, and drunkards, and murderers, if you are to enter eternal life; there is but one way and that is the way of grace.

Again, another influence of the fact mentioned in our text is that it forbids despair. Whoever you may be, if eternal life is to be had for nothing, you are not too poor to have it. It is impossible that you can have fallen too low for the gospel, for "Jesus Christ is able to save to the uttermost them that come unto God by him."

Next it inspires with gratitude, and that becomes the basis of holiness. They say that a free gospel will make men think lightly of sin. It is the death of sin, it is the life of virtue, it is the motive power of holiness, and when it comes into the soul it begets zeal for the Lord.

Then note again that the receipt of salvation without money and without price engenders in the soul the generous virtues. What do I mean by that? Why the man who is saved for nothing feels first with regard to his fellow-men that he must deal lovingly with them. Has God forgiven me? Then I can freely forgive those who have trespassed against me. He longs to see others saved, and therefore lays Himself out to bring them to Jesus Christ. Then as to our God, the free gifts of grace, working by the power and energy of the Holy Spirit, create in us the generous virtues towards God. When we know that Jesus has saved us we feel we could lay down our lives for him.

Lastly, beloved, I cannot think of anything that will make more devout worshippers in heaven than this. Every child of God will know eternally that he is saved by grace, grace, grace, from first to last, from beginning to end; and so without constraint, except that which is found within their own bosoms, all the redeemed will forever magnify the Lord in such notes as these, "Worthy art thou, O Lamb of God! For thou wast slain, and hast redeemed us unto God by thy blood, and hast made us kings and priests unto God."

May the Lord lead you all to receive his divine salvation "without money and without price."

Review Activities

Choose skills your student needs to review.

1. *Coordinating Conjunction*
   Name some coordinating conjunctions.

2. Write a sentence using a coordinating conjunction.

3. *Subordinating Conjunction*
   Name some subordinating conjunctions.

4. Write a sentence using a subordinating conjunction.

5. *Transitional Words*
   Name some transitional words or phrases.

6. *Outline*
   Read a short chapter from your science or history book. Write a topical outline.

---

1. Possible answers: and, or, but

2. Answers will vary.

3. Possible answers: since, although, when, because, unless, while, until

4. Answers will vary.

5. Possible answers: first, next, in the same way, as a result, in conclusion, for instance, otherwise, for this reason, for example, on the other hand

6. Answers will vary.

Note Taking Tips

1) Cultivate a learning attitude. Come prepared to listen and learn. The first preparation is to have your writing tools ready.

2) Avoid daydreaming and doodling. We can listen four times as fast as a speaker can talk. Taking notes will help you stay focused.

3) Begin taking notes immediately. If the lecture doesn't have a stated title, make up one of your own. Don't wait to begin writing when something "important" has been said.

4) Try to figure out the speaker's purpose. Is he trying to motivate, persuade, explain, or inform?

5) Listen for the speaker's stated organization of main points. Often a speaker will tell you the outline of his lecture.

6) Listen for transitional phrases alerting you that the speaker is starting a new point.

Transitional Words and Phrases

first	next	in the same way
as a result	in conclusion	for instance
otherwise	for this reason	for example
	on the other hand	

7) Do not try to write word for word statements, unless it is a line you would like to quote. Summarize the main points and write concisely, leaving out unnecessary words. This is one time when it is desirable to use incomplete sentences.

8) Jot down questions that come to your mind as you listen. You can find out the answers later.

9) Draw simple illustrations, charts, or diagrams if they help make the point being made clearer.

10) Read the notes you have taken within 24 hours. If you have taken notes of a lecture you will be tested on, you should recopy your notes, filling in the sketchy parts. Highlight those notes which are especially important to remember.

Answers:

4. b.

Fact: The Gifts of God are Free

I. Surprising nature of fact
  A. Man's relation to God and his wrong judgment of Him
    1. Man thinks God is hard master
    2. Fear of rejection for past sins
  B. The condition of man under the fall
    1. Man thinks he is doomed to toil for everything
    2. Sinner feels he must do something before he can receive gift
  C. Man Recollects the General Rule of Men
    1. Nothing for nothing
    2. Cannot believe truth
  D. Man's Natural Pride
    1. Woven into man's nature
      a. Keeps from seeing himself as a sinner
      b. Blinds him from the truth
    2. Best blessings are free
      a. Life, air, light
      b. Gift of grace

II. Necessity of fact
  A. Character of donor
  B. Value of the boon
  C. Extremity of human destitution

III. Salutary influence of fact
  A. Enables us to preach the gospel to every creature
  B. Excludes all pride
    1. The gate is straight
    2. Only one way, the way of grace
  C. Forbids despair
  D. Inspires with gratitude
    1. Basis of holiness
    2. Life of virtue
      a. Motive power of holiness
      b. Zeal for the Lord
  E. Engenders in the soul generous virtues
  F. Makes more devout worshippers

Assessment 3
(Lessons 19-25)

1. What is the rhyme scheme of this first verse from "The Lady of Shalott" by Alfred Lord Tennyson?

   On either side the river lie
   Long fields of barley and of rye,
   That clothe the wold, and meet the sky;
   And through the field the road runs by
   To many-towered Camelot;
   And up and down the people go,
   Gazing where the lilies blow
   Round an island there below,
   The island of Shalott.

2. What is the meter?

3. Define alliteration, assonance, and consonance. Write an example of each.

4. Write an example of the four types of sentences:

   declarative
   imperative
   interrogative
   exclamatory

5. Are the verbs in the following sentences transitive (**T**) or intransitive (**IT**)? If transitive, what is its object? Do any of the verbs have an indirect object?

   a. A duck sat on her nest.
   b. The hatching ducklings cracked their shells.
   c. One duckling gave her a fright.
   d. The big, ugly duckling felt sad.
   e. He grew into a beautiful swan.
   f. You should never judge a book by its cover.

---

1. aaaabcccb

2. unstressed, stressed (iambic)

3. alliteration - repeating the same consonant sound at the beginning of words. Ex: She sells seashells down by the seashore.

   assonance - repeating the same vowel sounds. Ex: G<u>i</u>ve me l<u>i</u>berty or g<u>i</u>ve me death.

   consonance - the repetition of consonant sounds not limited to the first letter of each word. Ex: But, children, you <u>sh</u>ould never let such angry pa<u>ss</u>ions ri<u>se</u>.

4.
   Ex: I am going to the circus. (declarative)
   Come with me. (imperative)
   Wouldn't you like to go? (interrogative)
   We will have a great time! (exclamatory)

5.
a. sat (intransitive verb)
b. cracked (transitive verb) shells (direct object)
c. gave (transitive verb) fright (direct object) her (indirect object)
d. felt (intransitive verb)
e. grew (intransitive verb)
f. judge (transitive verb) book (direct object)

6. Possible answers
   a. lunches
   b. ladies
   c. toys
   d. tomatoes
   e. pianos
   f. lives
   g. children
   h. moose

7.
a. fellow (predicate nominative)
b. Countess Amelia (predicate nominative)
c. unreasonable (predicate adjective)
d. Rudolf Rassendyl (predicate nominative)
e. fleshy (predicate adjective)
f. frequent (predicate adjective)
g. unfriendly (predicate adjective)

8. to come, to take, to double, to hint

9. hidden, Locked, running

6. Write a plural example for each of the following:

   a. noun ending in **ch**
   b. noun ending in consonant **y**
   c. noun ending in vowel **y**
   d. noun ending in vowel **o**
   e. noun ending in consonant **o**
   f. noun ending in **f**
   g. noun with an irregular plural form
   h. noun with same singular and plural form

7. Underline the predicate nominatives (**PN**) and predicate adjectives (**PA**) in the following sentences from *The Prisoner of Zenda*. Indicate if it is a predicate nominative or a predicate adjective:

   a. The prince was a tall, handsome young fellow.
   b. This lady was the Countess Amelia.
   c. I was not so unreasonable as to be prejudiced against the duke's keeper.
   d. I am Rudolf Rassendyl.
   e. The king's face was slightly more fleshy than mine.
   f. Duels were frequent among all the upper classes.
   g. The dark night suddenly seemed unfriendly.

8. Underline the infinitives in this paragraph from *The Prisoner of Zenda*:

   Dearly would he have liked to come with me, had I not utterly refused to take him. One man might escape notice, to double the party more than doubled the risk; and when he ventured to hint once again that my life was too valuable, I, sternly bade him be silent.

9. Underline the participles in this paragraph from *White Fang*:

   From hidden points of vantage the family watched the performance. But it was a fizzle. Locked in the yard and there deserted by the master, White Fang lay down and went to sleep. Once he got up and walked over to the trough for a drink of water. The chickens he calmly ignored. So far as he was concerned they did not exist. At four o'clock he executed a running jump, gained the roof of the chicken house and leaped to the ground outside, whence he sauntered gravely to the house.

10. Circle the gerunds in this paragraph from *White Fang*:

    It was the beginning of the end for White Fang - the ending of the old life and the reign of hate. A new and incomprehensibly fairer life was dawning. It required much thinking and endless patience on the part of Weedon Scott to accomplish this. And on the part of White Fang it required nothing less than a revolution. He had to ignore the urges and promptings of instinct and reason, defy experience, give the lie to life itself.

11. Write the comparative and superlative forms of these modifiers:

    a. red   d. heavy   f. good
    b. bad   e. easy   g. difficult
    c. gladly

12. Choose the correct word:

    a. He always tried to do his job (*well, good*).
    b. The warm coat felt (*well, good*) on the brisk fall day.
    c. We always eat (*well, good*) at summer camp.
    d. No one could play the piano as (*well, good*) as Sue.
    e. Peter felt (*bad, badly*) about missing the game.
    f. Keith's tooth ached (*bad, badly*).

13. Write sentences using the present, present participle, past, and past participle of the verbs *lay* and *lie*.

    Continued on next page.

---

10. beginning, ending, thinking, promptings

11.

	Comp.	Super.
a.	redder	reddest
b.	worse	worst
c.	more gladly	most gladly
d.	heavier	heaviest
e.	easier	easiest
f.	better	best
g.	more difficult	most difficult

12.
a. well
b. good
c. well
d. well
e. bad
f. badly

13.
Ex: lie, lying, lay, lain
Won't you *lie* down for awhile?
I will be *lying* down for a nap today.
I *lay* down for a nap yesterday.
I have *lain* down every day.

lay, laying, laid, laid
I *lay* the book on the table.
I saw her *laying* her book on her bed.
She *laid* it there yesterday.
She has *laid* it there before.

14.
Possible answers for *raise*:
Present: We proudly watch the honor guard *raise* the flag.

Present Participle: As the flag is *raising*, a cheer goes up around the crowd.

Past: After the flag is *raised*, everyone salutes.

Past Participle: The honor guard has *raised* the flag.

Possible answers for *rise*:
Present: It is customary to *rise* as the bride enters the church.

Present Participle: The old woman sits quietly, as the others are *rising*.

Past: Slowly, she *rose* to her feet.

Past Participle: When everyone had *risen*, the bride came down the aisle.

15.
Possible answers for *sit*:
Present: Would you like to *sit* in the sun?

Present Participle: Some were *sitting* in the shade.

Past: She *sat* down next to the young child.

Past Participle: I have *sat* with her before.

Possible answers for *set*:
Present: You can *set* aside all your fears.

Present Participle: She is *setting* the scene now.

Past: First, she *set* the table in center stage.

Past Participle: She has *set* the chairs on either side of the table.

14. Write sentences using the present, present participle, past, and past participle of the verbs *raise* and *rise*.

15. Write sentences using the present, present participle, past, and past participle of the verbs *sit* and *set*.

BOOK STUDY

on
Eric Liddell

Eric Liddell
By Catherine Swift
Published by Bethany
House

Summary

"Yet those who wait for the Lord will gain new strength. They will mount up with wings like eagles. They will run and not get tired, they will walk and not become weary."

Perhaps no one has come as close to literally living out this verse from Isaiah as the runner, Eric Liddell, introduced to our generation through the popular film *Chariots of Fire*. At the end of the movie we are told that Eric Liddell died in 1945 in China, twenty years after earning an Olympic gold medal in Paris. What happened during those twenty years? How did he come to die so young and so far away? To answer these questions we must go back some twenty years before the 1924 Olympic games.

Eric Liddell was born to missionary parents in Tientsin, China, in the year 1902. After surviving the dangers of the Boxer Rebellion, James and Mary Liddell with their two sons settled on the Great China Plain and began a missionary work among the Chinese peasants. Eric grew up speaking Chinese as well as English.

At the age of five, Eric was taken to England to be educated, as was the custom. At school, Eric developed into an excellent rugby and cricket player. He also began setting new track records. During these years, Eric's love for God continued as well as his interest in missions. Asked to join an evangelistic movement when in college, his reputation as a great athlete brought many to hear him speak.

Then in 1924, Eric was chosen as part of the British team competing in the Olympics in Paris, France as a sure winner of the 100 meter race. When the timetable of events was published, Eric was surprised to find that the 100 meters was scheduled on a Sunday. Eric felt the Sabbath was a day that belonged to God, not to sports, and so made the public declaration that was to stun the world, "I'm not running."

During that time, Eric learned the true meaning of "standing alone." Certainly there were those who admired him, but many of his countrymen considered him a traitor and he was ridiculed in the press. Although he wasn't their greatest hope, the authorities finally decided to put him in the 200 meter and the 400 meter races. This meant extra training for Eric. As history was to record, Eric came in third in the 200 meter and then stunned the world by by not only coming in first in the 400 meter but by setting a new world record.

After the Olympics, Eric was offered a post at the Tientsin College. He returned to China in 1925, where he eventually married. Later fighting broke out between the Chinese Nationalists and the Communists with Japan threatening an invasion of China. A major attack was launched by the Japanese in 1937 and by 1938 the Japanese army controlled most of eastern China. Events worsened and in 1941, a rumor circulated that the Japanese were going to send all missionaries to internment camps. Eric decided to send his wife and daughters to Canada for safety. In 1943, Eric along with the other remaining missionaries was sent to an internment camp. He never left the camp, dying of a brain tumor on February 21, 1945. There were 1800 people in the camp and everyone attended his funeral.

Perhaps Eric Liddell's life can best be summed up by a note that was thrust into his hand at the 1924 Olympic games. It read, "In the old book it says, "He that honors me, I will honor."

Colossians 3:23 says, "Whatever you do, do your work heartily as for the Lord." Eric Liddell felt that his running was "for the Lord" and he strove for excellency. Purpose to make this verse true in whatever you do.

Vocabulary

Find the word in its context. Reread the sentences before and after the word. What do you think the word means? Look up the word in the dictionary and write a clear, simple definition, and use it in a sentence.

1. a stream that flows into a larger river

1. tributary - (pg. 20)

2. an outdoor game played by two teams using a ball, bats, and wickets

2. cricket - (pg. 55)

3. vigorous actions for particular causes

3. crusades - (pg. 76)

4. disappointed; disenchanted

4. disillusioned - (pg. 152)

5. a fellow worker in the same profession

5. colleagues - (pg. 153)

Complete the sentences with the correct vocabulary word. OR Write your own sentences using the vocabulary words.

6. disillusioned

6. The young man began his career with great hopes, but he quickly became _____.

7. colleagues

7. Robert and his _____ petitioned for better working conditions.

8. crusades

8. The activist was involved in many _____ to stop abortion.

9. cricket

9. My friend taught me how to play _____ when I visited him in England.

10. tributary

10. Ships crossed the _____ before its final destination.

Activities

After reading *Eric Liddell* by Catherine Swift, complete two or three of the following activities of your choice. Complete the activities on a separate piece of paper.

1. *Eric Liddell* by Catherine Swift is one of the *Men of Faith* series published by Bethany House Publishers. Try to read more of the titles in this series, especially *Hudson Taylor*, biography of another missionary to China.

2. Cook a Chinese meal or go out to a Chinese restaurant.

3. Research the Boxer Rebellion. Who was involved? Why?

4. Why would the training for running the 400 meter be different than running the 100 meter? Try running each. Time your runs.

5. Note Eric Liddell's time for running the 400 meter. How does your time compare?

6. Research the history of the Olympic games. What events are included today?

7. Much has been written about the value of competition. Does competition have a positive or negative value? Write an essay stating your opinion.

8. Find out what the Scripture has to say about keeping the Sabbath. Write a paper about what you find that would help you defend your position if you are every challenged.

9. Watch the movie *Chariots of Fire* that tells about a short period in Eric Liddell's life. Do you think it gives an accurate portrayal of Eric Liddell?

✎ **Teacher's Note: We suggest you preview the movie to decide the appropriateness for your student.**

10. Find out some more about the Japanese occupation. How long did it last? It might be helpful to draw a timeline showing the highlights of Eric Liddell's last years and also some other major events of the World War II period.

11. What are some character qualities Eric developed as he trained to be a runner? (e.g. determination, self-discipline, etc.)

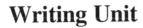

Writing Unit

Throughout this year, you have learned how to effectively express your thoughts and written about several topics. You have learned about grammar, spelling, and writing mechanics. For the next five weeks, you will be spending more time on various writing styles.

Here is the writing schedule you will be following:

Lesson 28   Narrative Paper
Lesson 29   Persuasive Paper
Lesson 30   Compare and Contrast Paper
Lessons 31 and 32   Research Paper

Having a model to follow helps make the writing process easier. Each writing assignment contains a sample paper for you to read.

JoAnna
start 9-25-02
finish by 10-1

Narrative Paper

Allow yourself one week to complete your Narrative Paper.

1. a. For this writing assignment, choose a topic designed to illustrate a point. This may be accomplished by invoking an emotional response, using humor, or by telling a story. Our sample paper is pleading an emotional response by using humor.

   b. The main element of a narrative is to give the details in the order in which they happened.

2. The first paragraph should contain your thesis statement. The thesis statement tells the main idea of your paper. This statement is again reworded in the last paragraph.

3. The middle paragraphs should each contain a related topic sentence. The other sentences within the paragraph should support the topic sentence.

4. Organize your writing plan before you begin writing.

5. The writing plan of the sample paper would like this:

   Title: Felines in Control

   Paragraph one (contains our thesis statement)
   Thesis statement: There has been a growing concern among the cat population that your humans are making attempts to train you to "come."

   Paragraph two
   Topic sentence: The human will not stop at this.

   Paragraph three
   Topic sentence: Do not use your weapon on the little humans.

   Reworded thesis statement: Remain in control and you will have a well-trained human, sure to serve you your entire life.

6. Write the first draft of your paper. Include your name and date on the top of the first page. Put it aside for a day before you begin revising it.

7. Use this check list to help you revise your first draft.

Check List
1) Read the paper.
2) Did you choose a good title?
3) Underline the thesis statement of the first paragraph twice. Does it clearly state the main idea of your paper?

---

8. After your revision, rewrite the paper. If you type the paper, be sure to double space.

The following is a sample narrative paper:

Felines in Control

There has been a growing concern among the cat population that your humans are making attempts to train you to "come." I urge you, fellow felines, do not give in.

The human will not stop at this. He will then want you to shake hands and catch frisbees. The human is widely known for his behavior of using *Lean Cuisines* to lure you. No matter how voracious your appetite, you must not let your human know this. Perhaps you did not eat your dinner last night because he had the audacity to give you...dry cat food...yuck! I plead with you; do not give in. The future cat generation depends on you. Your human will try again to entice you; this time with a tender voice saying, "Here, kitty, kitty." Beware of those candy-coated voices. Brother Tom ended up in a dress and bonnet when he last gave into those words. Finally, your human will try his last attempt. He will try to catch you bare-handed. There are several methods of escape. Scurry quickly away by darting to the right and left. Humans are slow and extremely dull. Or you may run in circles around your human and he will get dizzy and fall over. This last method is most entertaining to watch. If all else fails, reveal your weapon. Keep your claws sharpened and ready. This is sure to rid of even what the humans call the "man of the house."

However, I have one word of caution. Do not use your weapon on the little humans. They run to the one human we all fear most; the large female human, whom the little humans refer to as "Mommy." This human, who is usually so kind and gentle, and even warms your milk, turns into a raging lunatic, chasing you tirelessly with a broom, never to let you in the warm house again.

In closing, refuse to come when called. Remain in control and you will have a well-trained human, sure to serve you your entire life.

Persuasive Paper

Allow yourself one week to complete your Persuasive Paper.

1. a. For this writing assignment, choose a topic you feel strongly about. Our sample paper is on the support of creationism. The guidelines given will be on this topic.

   b. This paper will be a persuasive paper (Refer to Lesson 7) giving four supporting reasons why I have chosen Creation as the logical response to the origin of life.

   c. Write the paper in the first person (Refer to Lesson 2). Do not use the second person (you) at any time.

2. a. Each paragraph should have a topic sentence. The topic sentence states the subject you are going to develop in the paragraph.

   b. The other sentences in the paragraph (supporting sentences) will support the topic sentence. Often the topic sentence is the first sentence of the paragraph, but that is not always the case.

3. a. The first paragraph of your paper should contain your thesis statement.

   b. The thesis statement is a sentence that states the purpose, intent, or main idea of your paper. It is usually the last sentence in the first paragraph of your paper. The thesis statement should be again reworded in the last paragraph. This is usually the last sentence of the paragraph.

   c. In the following example, the thesis statement reads: The logical response to the origin of life is Creation.

   Notice that the statement does not list the reasons, but only states the main idea of the paper.

169

4. a. Check your thesis statement by asking the following questions:
   1) Is my thesis statement clearly worded?
   2) Can I develop the idea of the thesis statement satisfactorily?
   3) Does my thesis statement cover all my supporting material?

5. a. Let's get started. You have chosen a topic you feel strongly about. You have decided on four supporting reasons to persuade the reader that he should come to the same conclusion. You have written a thesis statement stating the purpose or main idea of your paper. In doing all this, you have developed a writing plan for your paper.

   b. The writing plan of the sample paper would look like this:

   Title: Creation, the Scientific Explanation

   Thesis statement: The logical response to the origin of life is Creation.

   Reason one
   Topic sentence: Fossil records do not show a series of change.

   Reason two
   Topic sentence: A master designer would choose similar organs for similar purposes.

   Reason three
   Topic sentence: Natural selection only operates within a kind.

   Reason four
   Topic sentence: There is no evidence of cosmic dust and the existence of meteoroids and comets points to a young Earth.

   Reworded Thesis Statement: I can logically conclude that Creation is the scientific explanation to the origin of life.

6.   Write the first draft of your paper. Write your name and date on the top of the first page. Remember to put your paper aside for a day before revising it.

7.   A bibliography completes the paper. Follow the example given at the end of this lesson.

8.   Use this checklist to help you revise your first draft:

Checklist

☐ Read the paper.

☐ Underline the topic sentence in each paragraph. Do the other sentences in the paragraph support the topic sentence?

☐ Underline the thesis statement twice. This should state the general idea of the paper. The thesis statement is usually the last sentence of the first paragraph.

☐ Find the reworded thesis statement in the last paragraph and underline it twice. This is usually the last sentence of the last paragraph. Does it repeat the thesis statement?

☐ Did you use any 2nd person personal pronouns (you, your, yours)? If so, take them out.

☐ Is there an interesting title?

☐ Did you include a bibliography?

☐ Does your paper have your name and the date at the top of the paper?

☐ Check the mechanics: spelling, punctuation, grammar.

---

9.   After you have make the corrections, rewrite the paper. Let someone else proofread your paper using the same checklist above. Write the final draft of your paper. If you type the paper, be sure to double space.

The following is a sample persuasive paper:

Creation, the Scientific Explanation

"Creationism is unscientific. Fossil records hold evidence of evolution." Upon closer examination of this evidence, I have discovered that the theory of evolution, in fact, is unscientific. The logical response to the origin of life is Creation.

The evolutionist declares that because the older rock strata contains only simple life forms; and the younger rock strata contains more recent, complex forms, evolution must be the scientific answer. However, an unbiased eye can see that although these fossils exist, there are no fossil records showing a series of gradual change of one kind of animal or plant to another. If evolution were true, this is what one would expect. Fossils have shown variations within a kind, but never stages of development into new kinds.

Secondly, the evolutionist states that because the similarities between ape and man include similarities in body form, the first stages of embryonic growth, the chemical make up of blood, and the reproductive cells, man must have evolved from the ape. To this statement, I suggest that only through a master designer could all living things be so similar. It is logical to use similar organs for similar purposes. It is improbable that this all came about as a matter of chance.

The obvious changes occurring in nature, either through a process of natural selection or mutation, support the theory of life evolving. True, changes in nature do occur and the process of natural selection does operate; however, these changes take place only within a kind. These changes are horizontal, not vertical. There has never been evidence of an upward change to more complex life forms. Natural selection operates to conserve the kinds of organisms as they were created. Mutations occur, but these changes are not beneficial. If all that the evolutionist claims is true, our world have to be very old. But evidence such as the lack of cosmic dust and ocean sediment; and the existence of meteoroids and comets points to a young Earth.

Finally, just as astronomers Sir Fred Hoyle and Chandra Wickramasingshe calculated the probability of life evolving from nonliving material to be one in ten to the 40,000 power, I can logically conclude that Creation is the scientific explanation to the origin of life.

Bibliography

Columbus, Charles E. Focus on Earth Science. Columbus:
    Meril Publishing Co., 1984.

Hyma, Albert and Mary Stanton. Streams of Civilization.
    Arlington Heights: Christian Liberty Press, 1992.

Peterson, Dennis R. Unlocking the Mysteries of Creation.
    Eldorado: Creation Resource Foundation, 1990.

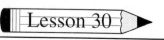
Compare and Contrast Paper

Allow yourself one week to complete your Compare and Contrast Paper.

1. a. For this week's writing assignment, choose two people, events, or ideas to compare and contrast. The sample paper is about two people.

   b. Do not write this paper in the first person (*I*) or refer to the second person (*you*).

2. a. The paper should be four paragraphs long following this format:
      1) First paragraph - introduce both people
      2) Second paragraph - short biography of first person
      3) Third paragraph - short biography of second person
      4) Fourth paragraph - state three ways these two people are alike or different

   b. Remember, the thesis statement should appear at the end of the first paragraph and again, reworded at the end of the paper.

3. Each paragraph should have a clear topic sentence, with the other sentences in the paragraph supporting it.

4. Develop your writing plan before you begin writing.

5. a. Here is the writing plan of the sample paper for this assignment:

Title: Callas and Andrews: Divas of Different Worlds

Thesis statement: Callas and Andrews will always be two
of the greatest shining stars in the world of music.

- First Paragraph
  Topic Sentence:
  > Maria Callas and Julie Andrews are two of the most
  > famous singers history has ever known.

  Supporting Sentences:
  > They revolutionized music
  > Unique voices
  > Both could sing and act

- Second Paragraph
  Topic Sentence:
  > Maria Callas, the world famous opera tragedian, brought
  > new life and meaning to operas that had been played for
  > decades.

  Supporting Sentences:
  > Best known Tosca and Norma
  > Fantastic dramatic actress

- Third Paragraph
  Topic Sentence:
  > Julie Andrews is probably best known for her role as
  > Maria Von Trapp in Walt Disney's famous "The Sound
  > of Music," but the talented actress/singer has had huge
  > success in playing a wide variety of other roles.

  Supporting Sentences:
  > Personable on stage
  > Sang for the Queen at age 12
  > Starred in movies and on Broadway
  > Has four octave range

- Fourth Paragraph
  Topic Sentence:
  > Famed for their singing, Callas and Andrews are similar
  > in some respects, but for the most part their two lives
  > differ greatly.

Supporting Sentences:
  Started their careers at young age - compare
  Maria: opera; Julie: Broadway - contrast
  Julie: happy family; Maria: unhappy, loneliness - contrast

b. Reword Thesis Statement: Even though their worlds were far apart, Maria Callas and Julie Andrews had one very important thing in common: the incredible vocal power that will not be quickly forgotten.

6. Collect your data and then write your first draft. Write your name and date on the top of the first page. Put the draft aside for a day, then begin the revision process.

7. Use this checklist to help you revise your first draft:

8. Bibliography (Review the example given at the end of this lesson.)

Checklist
☐ Read the paper.
☐ Did you choose a good title?
☐ Underline the thesis statement at the end of the first paragraph twice. Does it state the intent or purpose of your paper clearly?
☐ Underline the topic sentence of each paragraph. Do the other sentences in the paragraph support the topic sentence?
☐ Check mechanics: spelling, punctuation, grammar.

9. After revising your paper, let someone else read it using the same checklist as above. Listen to their suggestions and then write your final copy. If you type the paper, be sure to double space.

The following sample compare and contrast paper was written by student, Erin Welch.

Callas and Andrews: Divas of Different Worlds

Maria Callas and Julie Andrews are two of the most famous singers history has ever known. They are famous, not only for their singing abilities, but also for their wonderful acting techniques. Both revolutionized the world around them and set new and higher standards for future aspiring performers. Even though Callas performed in Opera and Andrews on Broadway, their voices were alike in the fact that they were unique. Andrews could easily have been an Opera great with her wonderfully high voice and coloratura runs. Callas, on the other hand, was a superb actress and could have started a second career in movies had she been so inclined. Callas and Andrews will always be two of the greatest shining stars in the world of music.

Maria Callas, the world famous opera tragedian, brought new life and meaning to operas that had been played for decades. Best known for her *Tosca* and *Norma*, Callas accomplished feats that no one past or present has ever been able to equal. Barker records that in one instance she was performing Wagner's *Die Walkure*, as the lead, Brunnhilde, when she was asked to take the place of the lead in Bellini's *I Puritani*. She had only a week to learn the part and, as the final dress rehearsal was the same day as *Die Walkure's* closing night, she went from singing, in the afternoon, one of the highest coloratura parts ever written, to singing, a few hours later, the heavy dramatic role of Brunnhilde. Not only did she have a voice that earned her encore after encore, Callas was also a fantastic dramatic actress. She believed that all the emotions and passions could be betrayed with small movements if the singer could only convey them through the voice. To the world of opera where big acting is expected, Callas stood alone, and the audience loved it. Callas revolutionized the world of opera and proved many times during her life that she was indeed the greatest soprano the world will ever know.

Julie Andrews is probably best known for her role as Maria Von Trapp in Walt Disney's famous *The Sound of Music*, but the talented actress/singer has had huge success in playing a wide variety of other roles. Andrews has starred in movies such as: *Mary Poppins, Thoroughly Modern Milly*, and *The Americanization of Emily*. She started her career at the age of five by performing occasionally with her mother and step-father, who were music hall performers. From there, she went on to sing for the future Queen Mother Elizabeth and Princess Margaret at the age of twelve. In America she starred in many

Broadway plays including *Camelot, My Fair Lady*, and *Cinderella* to name just a few. Happily married with five children, Julie Andrews is the Goodwill Ambassador for the United Nations Development Fund for Women. She also supports many charity organizations which help underprivileged children. Andrews' four octave range and beautiful voice have helped her become one of the most beloved Broadway stars of all times.

Famed for their singing, Callas and Andrews are similar in some respects, but for the most part, their two lives differ greatly. Both started their careers at a very young age. Callas performed her first opera when she was sixteen and Andrews became a Broadway star at the age of nineteen. In contrast, the type of music they sang is worlds removed from each other. Callas specialized in tragic opera and beautifully translated the passions through the wonderful timber of her voice. Antithetically, Andrews was the queen of romantic and light comedy. The two women's personal lives differ greatly also. Andrews has been pleasantly married for over twenty years with a family of five and, though advancing in age, is still performing on Broadway and making recordings. Callas, on the other hand, experienced one misfortune after another and was very unhappy. Although their worlds are far apart, Maria Callas and Julie Andrews have one very important thing in common: an incredible vocal power which will not be quickly forgotten.

Bibliography

Barker, Frank. The Incomparable Callas. Hayes, England: EMI Records Ltd., 1987.

Stassinopoulos, Arianna. Maria Callas: The Woman Behind the Legend. New York: Simon and Schuster, 1981.

Windeler, Robert. Julie Andrews: A Biography. Toronto: Longman's Canada Limited, 1970.

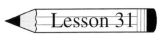
Research Paper

The final writing assignment in the unit will be the research paper. This paper should be about five typed pages, double spaced. You are given two weeks to complete it. Our sample paper is on the history of opera. Choose one of the following suggestions or another topic of your choice.

1) a historical figure
2) a country
3) an animal
4) a historical event
5) a sport
6) an invention
7) space
8) weather
9) ocean
10) transportation

Week 1

1. Before you begin writing, gather your sources. Find as many varied sources as you can. Using your sources, write down facts that you think should be in your paper. As you do this, keep a list of the works you plan to use. Using index cards, list each source on an individual card. This will be helpful when you write the bibliography.

(Title)	Mountain Climbing
(Author)	Aileen Dover
(Publisher)	Good Books Press
(Copyright Year)	1991

2. As you take notes, be careful not to copy the exact words of the text. This is called plagiarism. A good report will be written in your own words.

3. Once you have gathered your information, it is time to develop your thesis statement and writing plan. The following is the outline developed for the sample paper for this assignment.

Title: Opera: "As Time Goes By"

Thesis Statement: A short walk through history will show something of the great composers, great singers, and great operas that embellish and enhance the glorious history of opera.

   I. Creation to the present age
      A. Grown and evolved in both shape and sound
      B. Produced a new type of opera and new singers to sing in them
      C. Immortalized through constant performance

  II. The origin of music
      A. The earliest reference
      B. Thirteenth century BC
      C. David and Solomon
      D. Early church
      E. AD 325

 III. The Middle Ages introduced polyphony
      A. Notre Dame started the motet
      B. Well trained choirs
      C. In Italy, *ars nova* replaces the *ars antiqua* in the fourteenth century

 IV. The Renaissance
      A. *Ars nova* music developed into the freer form of *chansons*
      B. The invention of the printing press
      C. *Madrigals* and *ayres*

  V. The Baroque Period - opera polished and developed
      A. The oldest surviving opera
      B. Monteverdi's *Orfeo* (1607).
      C. The era of the virtuoso
      D. Bach, Handel, Scarlati, and others

 VI. The 1700's a time of Classicism and Reason
      A. Music was orderly and restrained
      B. Mozart, possibly the greatest melody writer the world will ever know, was born
      C. Gluck, Haydn, and Clementi also wrote great operas

VII.   The Romantic era
       A. Beethoven, Bizet, Gounod, Rossini, Sullivan,
          Tchaikovsky, Verdi, and Wagner
       B. A new kind of opera comes into being
       C. The age of beautiful singing
       D. Rossini example of *bel canto*

VIII. The age of the singer
       A. Many opera singers have risen up to shine in the
          limelight
       B. They have revealed the forgotten qualities of opera
       C. Opera has lasted through the ages
       D. An opera singer today can make anywhere from
          between seven thousand to seventy thousand dollars
          per performance
       E. With hundreds of opera houses all over the United
          States alone the future looks very bright for the singer

IX.   Opera as spoof
       A. Limited knowledge of opera
       B. The music of opera
       C. The history of opera stretches through time

Once you have developed your thesis statement and
organized your writing plan, writing the paper becomes much
easier.

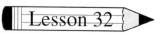
Week Two

1. Begin writing the first draft of your paper. When you have completed it, put it aside until the next day.

2. As you begin the revision process, remember this is the way writers improve their work. Use the following checklist:

Checklist
☐ Read the entire paper for content. Did you follow your writing plan? Did you include your list of sources accurately?
☐ Did you choose an interesting title?
☐ Underline the these statement twice. Did you end with a reworded thesis statement? Underline it twice.
☐ Would your introductory paragraph arouse a reader's interest?
☐ Does the concluding paragraph help the reader understand the significance of what you have written?
☐ Underline the topic sentence of each paragraph. Are the topic sentences supported by the other sentences in the paragraph?
☐ Did you use varied sentence lengths?
☐ Does each paragraph naturally flow to the next?
☐ Include a bibliography.
☐ Read the paper once more checking the mechanics: spelling, punctuation, and grammar.

3. After completing this checklist, your paper should have marks all over it showing your corrections and changes. That is good. It means you are working at improving your writing. You might find it helpful to get an outside opinion of your paper at this time. Consider any suggestions you receive and choose to use those you agree with.

4. Write or type a final copy of your research paper. This paper should have a cover sheet. Follow this example.

Opera: "As Time Goes By"

Erin Welch
Teacher's Name
Course Name
Date

This is a sample Research Paper.

Opera: "As Time Goes By"

The history of the opera stretches from shortly after Creation to the present age. From the first strains of monophonic music to ballad singers of the Renaissance Age to modern opera, music and then opera has grown and evolved in both shape and sound. Thousands of operas have been written and millions of people have enjoyed them live, on television, on cassette tape or on C.D. Each new age produced a new type of opera and new singers to sing them. Some have passed into oblivion, never to be revived again, but many live forever in the audiences' hearts and will be revised and resung for generations to come. Out of these, names such as *Tosca, Madame Butterfly*, and *The Marriage of Figaro* will forever be imprinted on the world's memory as "the sound of great opera." Not only are the operas immortalized through constant performances, but the names of the singers themselves have been forever etched into the rock of time as a reminder of the heights of accomplishment they achieved. A short walk through history will show something of the great composers, great singers, and great operas that embellish and enhance the glorious history of opera.

The history of opera has its roots in the origin of music, shortly after the beginning of time. The earliest reference is found in Genesis 4:21 where it speaks of Jubal, the father of music. Later, in what was believed to be the thirteenth century BC, Moses and the Israelites sang praises to God for rescuing them from the Egyptians. Many songs were written after that and sung by the Jews in worship and thanksgiving to the Lord. The ancient Romans and Greeks were also know to have sung to their pagan idols. David, author of most of the book of Psalms (songs) and the second king of Israel, wrote many songs in worship of God to be sung in the Tabernacle during the worship service. His son Solomon, the wisest man who ever lived, was known to have written one thousand and five songs. With the advent of Christianity, the early church continued the Jewish tradition of singing and chanting the Psalms of David. The influence of Christian music spread throughout the ancient world when, in AD 325, Emperor Constantine proclaimed Christianity the official religion of the Roman Empire.

Until the ninth century music was only monophonic - literally, a single line of sound, but with the Middle Ages came polyphony or multi-voiced music. The church of Notre Dame in France became the leader of this new phase in music, and it was there that the *motet*, a polyphonic composition, usually in three parts, was first invented. The monophonic sounds of troubadours and congregational singing were largely replaced by well trained choirs that grew in size as time went on. In Italy meanwhile, *ars nova* (Latin, "new art"), identified by its greater complexity and varied rhythmic patterns, was taking root and would soon spread to France in the fourteenth century to replace the *ars antiqua or* "old art."

In the fifteenth century, following close on the heels of the Middle Ages came what Derrick Henry calls the richest period of music in history, the Renaissance. From the now old *ars nova* music developed into the freer form of *chansons*, three part music, one part sung and the other two instrumental. This new music spread rapidly aided by the invention of the printing press in 1450. New techniques grew with astonishing rapidity and a new kind of harmonics began to take the stage. *Madrigals*, five or six voice singing, and *ayres*, solo singing with usually lute accompaniment, were embraced by the populace and quickly grew in intricacy. Then finally, during the late Renaissance, opera was born.

Opera, the child of the Renaissance, was polished and developed in the next age: the Baroque. Many of the great opera composers were born in this period and contributed much to the evolution of opera. The oldest surviving opera is Jacopo Peri's *Euridice* (1600), however Monteverdi's *Orfeo* (1607) became the structure that opera was built on. Henry Purcell wrote several 'semi- operas' during this time among which are *The Fairy Queen* and *King Arthur*. The Baroque era became the era of the virtuoso. Singers and performers were encouraged to stretch themselves and their talents to the limit. Bach, Handel, Scarlati and others like them wrote beautiful soaring music for both the singer and the orchestra; but as the pendulum of time continued to swing, the emphasis of music began to leave the Baroque, with all its emphasis of grandeur and obedience, and move on to the age of Enlightenment, the Classical era.

Music had now entered the 1700's, a time of Classicism and Reason. Music was orderly and restrained, and it was during this time that Mozart was born. The operas he wrote are still some of the best sellers today. Who has not heard of *Die Zauberflote (The Magic Flute)* or *Le Nozze di Figaro (The Marriage of Figaro)*? Classics World records that Mozart was a composer whose genius has never been equaled. He wrote music, complete and perfect down to the last notation, as fast as he could think, and his speed continues to astonish scholars today. Over the short period of his life, he composed over 600 works, including 21 stage and opera works, 15 Masses, over 50 symphonies, 25 piano concertos, 12 violin concertos, 27 concert arias, 17 piano sonatas, 26 string quartets . . . the list seems endless. Mozart was the greatest melody writer the world has ever know. In his own time, he was the master of counterpoint and fugue; his operas range from comic to tragic masterpieces. His Requiem, stands with Bach's St. Matthew Passion as the supreme example of vocal music. Mozart, though, was not alone in this age of fabulous composers, Gluck, Haydn, and Clementi also wrote great operas and music that will never die. Their music shows the restraint and orderliness of their time. Soon after though, the age of Reason would give way to its opposite: the Romantic age.

The power of nature and human emotion became the central themes of the Romantic era. This is evidenced in the music of Beethoven, Bizet, Gounod, Rossini, Sullivan, Tchaikovsky, Verdi, and Wagner, just a few of the great composers of this era. Their operas *Fidelio, Carmen, Romeo et Juliette, Il Barbiere di Siviglia, The Mikado, Pique Dame, Aida* and *Der Ring des Nibelungen* are still performed and loved world wide. With the large casts and rich staging of the Romantic era came the age of *bel canto* or beautiful singing. The singers would add many embellishments (trills, runs) that the composer had not originally put into his work. The audiences loved this, but many of the composers found it annoying. An amusing story illustrating this is told by Stephen M. Stroff in his book *Opera*. It seems that Adelina Patti, the teenage Queen of Song, was presented to Rossini at his home one day. She thought to please him by singing an aria from his opera *Il Barbierre di Siviglia*. Like all the singers of that time, she generously embellished the music with cadenzas and high notes.

From the Romantic age, opera has now entered the age of the singer. Over the past few decades many opera singers have risen up to shine in the limelight, and through their singing they have brought the world of opera somewhat closer to the common man and made it a little easier for him to understand and enjoy it. Opera has lasted through the ages and will continue to entertain and thrill thousands of eager audiences. Opera houses such as the New York Metropolitan are still thriving and producing many different operas each year. *The Encyclopedia of Careers* says that formal education does not seem to be a requirement for singers; however it can be very useful. In addition to learning at schools of music, many singers take private lessons from voice teachers who help them develop their voices. The main qualification for employment is talent, and since there is a large amount of people pursuing musical careers, competition can be very stiff. While the available jobs for singers appears to be growing, the salary is highly dependent on the professional reputation of the singer.

Very few singers achieve the glamorous jobs and very lucrative contracts of the opera diva. The famous opera singer makes $8,000 and more per performance, while the opera chorus singer earns $600 to $800 a week. A classical soloist can make between $2,000 and $3,000 a performance with the choristers receiving around $70 per performance. With hundreds of opera houses all over the United States alone, the future looks very bright for the singer.

Opera has been the spoof of many a comedienne or cartoon, the wide mouths of singers, the winged helmet and breastplate, the huge old sopranos playing dainty young girls, all this can bring a laugh from an audience. John Welch, a local engineer, says that the only reason he knows *The Marriage of Figaro* is an opera is from watching Walt Disney's cartoon with the singing whale. Many people's knowledge of opera is limited to what they have heard in cartoons, and thus they have missed the joy of opera, being sidetracked by its comic side. Yes, opera plots are generally silly and convoluted with a tragic death scene thrown in at the end, but the music of opera is what has carried it through the ages. The sustained high E's and F's of the sopranos, the wonderful soaring melodies, the closely woven harmonies, these are what make opera worthwhile listening. The names of Maria Callas, Luciano Pavorotti, Joan Sutherland, and Enrico Caruso are immortalized in history with the feats they accomplished and the fame they won. As Frank Barker says, they have revealed the forgotten qualities of opera just as the restoration of old paintings shows the true colors of the masters. From the Psalms of David to the silky notes of Kathleen Battle today, the history of opera stretches through time, a glorious reminder of past ages and a standard for what is to come.

Bibliography

Barker, Frank. The Incomparable Callas. Hayes, England: EMI Records Ltd., 1987.

BMG Music (1995). "Classics World Biography: Wolfgang Amadeus Mozart 1756-1791." n.pag. Online. Internet. 7 April 1997. Available: www.classicalmus.com.

Cosgrove, Holli R. and J.G. Ferguson. "Singers." *Encyclopedia of Careers and Vocational Guidance*, 1997.

Grout, Donald Jay. A History of Western Music. New York: W. W. Norton, 1960.

Henry, Derrick. The Listener's Guide to Medieval and Renaissance Music. New York: Quarto Marketing Ltd., 1983.

Mann, William. James Galway's Music in Time. New York: Mitchell Beazley, 1982.

Stanley, John. "Classical Music." Reader's Digest June, 1944: 22-25.

Wechsburg, Joseph. *The Opera*. New York: Macmillan, 1972.

Welch, John. personal interview by Erin Welch. 2 April 1997.

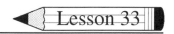

✎ Teacher's Note: As your student completes each lesson, choose skills from the *Review Activities* that he needs. The *Review Activities* follow each lesson.

How firm a foundation, ye saints of the Lord,
Is laid for your faith in His excellent Word!
What more can He say than to you He hath said,
To you who for refuge to Jesus have fled?

"Fear not, I am with thee; O be not dismayed,
For I am thy God, and will still give thee aid;
I'll strengthen thee, help thee, and cause thee to stand,
Upheld by My righteous omnipotent hand."

"When through fiery trials thy pathway shall lie,
My grace, all sufficient, shall be thy supply.
The flame shall not hurt thee; I only design
Thy dross to consume and thy gold to refine."

"The soul that on Jesus hath leaned for repose
I will not, I will not desert to its foes;
That soul, though all hell should endeavor to shake,
I'll never, no never, no, never forsake!"

"How Firm a Foundation," "K" in *Rippon's
Selection of Hymns from the Best Authors*, 1787.

1. a. Read the poem aloud. This is a hymn you may have heard sung before. It was written 200 years ago.

   b. As in much poetry, the first letter in each line is capitalized even if it does not begin a new sentence. Write the hymn from dictation. Compare to the model and correct. Add any misspelled words to your *Personal Spelling List*.

   c. Take a spelling test of the remaining 20 words from the *Commonly Misspelled Words List*. Add any words you misspell to your *Personal Spelling List* and study the list this week.

   d. Why are there quotation marks around the second through fourth verses?

   e. Begin memorizing the hymn. You will recite or write it from memory on Day 5.

1.
d. The hymnist is writing as if God were speaking.

2.

a. *dismayed* - deprived of courage

omnipotent - possessing unlimited powers

design - to purpose or intend

dross - a wasten product taken off molten metal during smelting

repose - lying at rest

endeavor - to try

forsake - to depart from

c. Possible answer:

How Firm a Foundation:

The saints of the Lord have a firm foundation on His Word. He cannot say more than He has already said to you who have sought refuge in Jesus.

God has said, "Do not fear for I am with you. Do not be dismayed for I am your God and will give you aid. I will strengthen you, help you and cause you to stand. I will uphold you with my righteous omnipotent hand."

"When you go through fiery trials, my sufficient grace will be supplied to you. The flames will not hurt you, my only design is to consume your dross and refine you like gold."

"I will not desert the soul that leans on Jesus for repose. Even if all hell should endeavor to shake that soul, I will never, never forsake it."

3.

a. aabb - unstressed,

b. unstressed, stressed (anapestic)

2. a. Vocabulary Builder - dismayed, omnipotent, design, dross, repose, endeavor, forsake

Write a dictionary sounding definition for each word using the context clues and your own knowledge. Look up the words in the *Glossary* and then write a sentence using each word.

b. This poem is a hymn set to music. Sing the hymn if you know the tune.

c. Prose is the ordinary form of spoken or written language. Rewrite this poem in prose.

d. Continue your memorization.

3. a. Scan the poem. What is its rhyme scheme? (Refer to Lesson 19.)

b. Determine the metrical pattern of the poem. What foot does it have?

c. Choose another hymn or poem and scan it to determine its rhyme scheme and metrical pattern.

d. Continue your memorization.

4. a. The writer of this poem chose the theme of faith in God's love and care, even through trials. Look up the following verses to see how the poet weaves these truths throughout the poem:

1) Psalm 9:9-10
2) Psalm 32:6-7
3) Psalm 46:1-3
4) Psalm 91:9-10
5) Lamentations 3:19-25
6) II Corinthians 12:9
7) I Peter 1:6-9

Can you find any others?

b. Writing **structural poems** (poems that follow a common
    form) is good practice. It will help you choose strong
    modifiers and to say what you need to say using just a few
    words. One form of structural poetry is called **diamante**. It
    takes its name from the diamond shape it forms. This is the
    pattern for a diamante:

Line 1 - Write a noun.

Line 2 - Write two adjectives describing the noun on Line 1.

Line 3 - Write three participles ending in **-ing** describing
         the word on Line 1.

Line 4 - Write two nouns relating to or describing the word
         on Line 1 and two nouns that relate to or describe
         the antonym on Line 7.

Line 5 - Write three participles ending in **-ing** that describe
         the word on Line 7.

Line 6 - Write two adjectives describing the word on Line 7.

Line 7 - Write an antonym for the word on Line 1.

Here is an example of a diamante taking the theme of this
week's poem:

fear

horrid, dreadful

panicking, gasping, running

fright, doubt, hope, faith

hoping, relying, depending

dependable, honest

trust

Write a diamante poem using these two antonyms: lost/ found.

c. Another poetry form is the **cinquain**. It follows this pattern:

Line 1 - Write a one-word topic.

Line 2 - Write two adjectives, and separate them by a comma.

Line 3 - Write three verbs that tell what the topic on Line 1 does. Separate them by commas.

Line 4 - Write a thought about the word you wrote on Line 1. This should be a short phrase (four to five words) expressing a feeling.

Line 5 - Repeat the word you wrote on Line 1 or write down a synonym or a related word.

Ex:

Scripture
True, Unchanging
Teaching, Correcting, Reproving
A letter from God
Bible

Write a cinquain.

d. Continue your memorization.

5. a. Take a spelling test using the words you misspelled this week.

b. Scan this hymn and determine the rhyme scheme and metrical pattern:

Come, Thou Fount of every blessing
Tune my heart to sing Thy grace;
Streams of mercy, never ceasing,
Call for songs of loudest praise.
Teach me some melodious sonnet,
Sung by flaming tongues above;
Praise His name—I'm fixed upon it—
Name of God's redeeming love.

To grace how great a debtor
Daily I'm constrained to be!
Let Thy goodness, like a fetter,
Bind my wandering heart to Thee:
Prone to wander, Lord, I feel it,
Prone to leave the God I love;
Here's my heart, O take and seal it;
Seal it for Thy courts above.

(Robert Robinson)

c. Write the above hymn in prose.

d. Choose a theme from the hymn and write either a cinquain or a diamante poem.

e. Recite or write the hymn from memory.

f. Choose skills from the *Review Activities* on the next page.

5.

b. ababcdcd - unstressed, unstressed, stressed (anapestic)

c. Possible answer:
Come, Thou Fount of Every Blessing
Come, You the source of every blessing and tune my heart to sing of your grace. Your mercy never ceases and calls for loud songs of praise. Teach me some melodious sonnet that is sung above by flaming tongues. I praise His name for I am fixed upon that name, God's redeeming love. Daily I am constrained to be a great debtor to grace. Let Your goodness bind my heart to you like a fetter. I feel I am prone to wander and leave the God I love. Here is my heart, take and seal it.

Review Activities

Choose skills your student needs to review.

1. *Rhyme Scheme and Meter*
   Scan the first verse of this poem by William Wordsworth and determine its rhyme scheme and meter:

   I wondered lonely as a cloud
   That floats on high o'er vales and hills,
   When all at once I saw a crowd,—
   A host, of golden daffodils
   Beside the lake, beneath the trees,
   Fluttering and dancing in the breeze.

2. *Simile*
   What is the simile?

1. ababcc
   unstressed, stressed
   (iambic)

2. lonely as a cloud

Beautiful Things

Beautiful faces are those that wear—
It matters little if dark or fair—
Whole-souled honesty printed there.

Beautiful eyes are those that show,
Like crystal panes where hearthfires glow,
Beautiful thoughts that burn below.

Beautiful lips are those whose words
Leap from the heart like songs of birds,
Yet whose utterance prudence girds.

Ellen P. Allerton

1. a. Listen to the first three verses of "Beautiful Things," a poem written by Ellen P. Allerton. This poem also begins each line with a capital letter. Write the poem from dictation. Compare to the model and make any needed corrections. If you misspelled any words, add them to your *Personal Spelling List.*

   b. Take a review spelling test of any words your teacher chooses from your *Personal Spelling List.*

   c. What is the rhyme scheme of this poem? (Refer to Lesson 19, Day 2.)

   d. What is the meter of the poem? (Refer to Lesson 19, Day 3.)

   e. A simile is a comparison made between two things that are similar yet very different, using the words *like* or *as* to compare them. Find the two similes in this poem.

2. a. Vocabulary Builder - prudence

   Write a dictionary sounding definition for this word using the context clues and your own knowledge. Look it up in the *Glossary* and then write a sentence using the word.

1.
c. aaa

d. stressed, unstressed, unstressed (dactylic)

e. like crystal panes
like songs of birds

2.
a. *prudence* - cautious, practical wisdom

b. One way to practice writing poetry is to use another poem as a model. You first must scan the poem to find out its rhyme scheme and meter. In Lesson 19 we analyzed "Mary Had a Little Lamb." The rhyme scheme was **abab** and it had a meter of DUMM-de, DUMM-de.

Here is the first verse of a poem by Elizabeth Turner that somewhat follows "Mary Had a Little Lamb":

Mary had a little bird
With feathers bright and yellow
Slender legs—upon my word
He was a pretty fellow.

Write your own verse using "Mary Had a Little Lamb" as your model.

c. In the poem "Beautiful Things," the poet is describing a beautiful person. Using the poem as a model, write two more verses. Begin your first verse, "Beautiful hands are those that...." Begin your second verse, "Beautiful feet are those that...."

3. a. Write the following poem from dictation:

I come more softly than a bird,
And lovely as a flower;
I sometimes last from year to year
And sometimes but an hour.
I stop the swiftest railroad train
Or break the stoutest tree.
And yet I am afraid of fire
And children play with me.

3.

b. snow

b. This is an example of a riddle poem. In fact, it is entitled "Rhyming Riddle." In a riddle poem, the poet tells the reader what his subject is like but never tells what it is. They are usually more riddle than poem, but with some care, can be written as good poetry. Riddle poems are fun to solve and fun to write. You will find that your use of imagery will be sharpened as you practice writing this type of poem. Can you solve the "Rhyming Riddle" by Mary Austin?

c. Here's a riddle poem that is more difficult to solve. It was written by Emily Dickinson. Can you solve it?

I like to see it lap the miles,
And lick the valleys up,
And stop to feed itself at tanks;
And then, prodigious, step

Around a pile of mountains,
And, supercilious, peer
In shanties by the sides of roads;
And then a quarry pare

To fit its sides, and crawl between,
Complaining all the while
In horrid, hooting stanza;
Then chase itself downhill

And neigh like Boanerges;
Then, punctual as a star,
Stop—docile and omnipotent—
At its own stable door.

d. To write your own riddle poem, begin by choosing an object. Think about what color it is, how it acts, what shape it is, how it sounds, smells, or tastes. Then compare it with something that it is like, but still very different from. It is a good idea to make more than one comparison. For example, in the "Rhyming Riddle" the poet describes snow as being as soft as a bird and as lovely as a flower as well as telling you what it can do. Write your own riddle poem.

3.
c. a locomotive

4. a. Another easy form of poetry is the limerick.

The limerick basically follows this form:

Lines 1, 2, and 5 rhyme.
Lines 3 and 4 rhyme.

Lines 1, 2, and 5 usually have from 8 to 10 syllables.
Lines 3 and 4 usually have from 5 to 7 syllables.

Read the following limerick:

There was a Young Lady whose Nose
continually prospers and grows;
When it grew out of sight,
She exclaimed in a fright,
"Oh! Farewell to the end of my Nose!"

(Edward Lear)

Write a limerick.

b. The following is the beginning of a poem written by Christina Rossetti describing the colors.

What is pink? A rose is pink
By the fountain's brink.
What is red? A poppy's red
In its barley bed.
What is blue? The sky is blue
Where the clouds float through.

Choose two more colors and continue the poem following the same structure.

c. This poem, also by Christina Rossetti, describes adjectives:

What are heavy? Sea-sand and sorrow;
What are brief? Today and tomorrow;
What are frail? Spring blossoms and youth;
What are deep? The ocean and truth.

Model the poem by choosing two more adjectives to describe.

5. a. Take a final spelling test.

   b. Here are the first two verses of a poem called "Months of the Year" by Sara Coleridge. Write a third verse for it.

   January brings the snow,
   makes our feet and fingers glow.

   February brings the rain,
   Thaws the frozen lake again.

   March brings breezes loud and shrill,
   Stirs the dancing daffodil.

   c. This is the first verse of a poem called "When I Get Time" written by Thomas L. Masson. Write a third verse for it.

   When I get time—
   I know what I shall do;
   I'll cut the leaves of all my books
   And read them through and through.

   When I get time—
   I'll write some letters then
   That I have owed for weeks and weeks
   to many, many men.

   d. Write another riddle poem.

   e. For a *Review Activity* of this lesson, try writing any kind of poetry of your choice.

Assessment 4
(Lessons 28 - 34)

1. Take a spelling test of any words your teacher chooses from the *Commonly Misspelled Words List.*

2. What is a thesis statement?

3. Underline the topic sentence of this paragraph from a sermon by Charles Spurgeon.

> Another matter helps man into this difficulty, namely, his natural pride. He does not like to be a pauper before God. Pride is woven into man's nature. We do not like to be saved by charity, and so have no corner in which to sit and boast. You insult a moral man if you tell him that he must be saved in the same way as a thief or murderer, yet this is not more than the truth.

4. If one of the sources for your research paper was the book, *The Biblical Basis for Modern Science* by Henry M. Morris, how would you list it in a bibliography? The book was published by Baker Book House in 1984.

5. Scan the following poem by Hamlin Garland for rhyme scheme and meter:

> The mountains they are silent folk,
> They stand afar—alone;
> And the clouds that kiss their brows at night
> Hear neither sigh nor groan.

6. Is there an example of simile or metaphor in this poem?

---

2. thesis statement - a sentence that states the purpose, intent, or main idea of your paper

3. <u>Another matter helps man into this difficulty, namely, his natural pride.</u>

4. Morris, Henry M. <u>The Biblical Basis for Modern Science</u>. Grand Rapids: Baker Book House, 1984.

5. abcb
unstressed, stressed (iambic)

6. metaphor - The mountains they are silent folk

✎ Teacher's Note: clouds that kiss their brows; hear - This is called personification.

7. Copy this paragraph from *The Black Arrow*:

Dick led the way upstairs and along the corridor. In the brown chamber the rope had been made fast to the frame of an exceeding heavy and ancient bed. It had not been detached, and Dick, taking the coil to the window, began to lower it slowly and cautiously into the darkness of the night. Joan stood by.

   a. Underline the subject of each sentence once and the verb or verb phrase twice.
   b. Circle the adverbs and adjectives.
   c. Put parentheses around the prepositional phrases.
   d. Box in the conjunctions.

8. Copy the following paragraphs from *A Man Called Peter*. Correct the capitalization and punctuation.

the emerald isle where a tender took off passengers for belfast looked good to me. any kind of land would have looked good. i said as much.
   that catherine shows just how sick you are commented peter.
   what do you mean
   you are seeing that land through jaundiced eyes or it would not look good. thats ireland.
   how i wondered loftily could any intelligent man be so prejudiced

7.

a. Dick led; rope had been made; it had not been detached; Dick began; Joan stood

b. adverbs: upstairs, fast, exceeding, slowly, cautiously, by

   adjectives: brown, heavy, ancient

c. along the corridor, in the brown chamber, to the frame, of an exceeding heavy and ancient bed, to the window, into the darkness, of the night

d. and, and, and, and

8.

The Emerald Isle, where a tender took off passengers for Belfast, looked good to me. Any kind of land would have looked good. I said as much.
   "That, Catherine, shows just how sick you are," commented Peter.
   "What do you mean?"
   "You are seeing that land through jaundiced eyes or it would not look good. That's Ireland."
   "How," I wondered loftily, "Could any intelligent man be so prejudiced?"

9. Answers will vary, but this is how Miss St. John wrote it:

The Roman guard was relieved by a great fierce brute of a man who sat with his back to the wall, scowling and picking his teeth. Paul greeted him courteously, and the talk flowed on, but Onesimus lost the thread. By the light of a smoky lamp he was watching the faces of the little company, urgent and troubled. There was a thin, dedicated-looking young man called Timothy, whose eyes blazed with love as he watched the apostle, and another older man, called Epaphroditus, who seemed to be convalescing from a serious illness. A third, with Jewish features, sat humbly in the background and said very little - probably a servant, thought Onesimus sleepily and wondered how long they would all go on talking.

Your student's work will probably differ somewhat.

9. The following paragraph from *Twice Freed* has been simplified. Combine sentences to make it more interesting to read:

The Roman guard was relieved by a great fierce brute of a man. The man sat with his back to the wall. The man was scowling. The man was picking his teeth. Paul greeted him courteously. The talk flowed on. Onesimus lost the thread. He could see by the light of a smoky lamp. He was watching the faces of the little company. The company was urgent and troubled. There was a thin, dedicated-looking young man. The young man was called Timothy. Timothy's eyes blazed with love. He watched the apostle. There was another older man. He was called Epaphroditus. He seemed to be convalescing from a serious illness. There was a third man. He had Jewish features. He sat humbly in the background. He said very little. Onesimus sleepily thought he was probably a servant. Onesimus wondered how long they would all go on talking.

BOOK STUDY

on
God's Smuggler

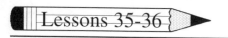
God's Smuggler
**By Brother Andrew with
John and Elizabeth Sherrill
Published by Penguin
Group**

Summary

Adventure! Andrew seemed to always be craving adventure. Even as a small boy, when he could not find any, he created his own. Then the Nazis invaded his homeland of Holland. Finally Andrew was experiencing all the adventure he wanted as he fought his own underground war. This excitement grew old when poverty and hunger began to take its toll on his family and country. At last the war ended and Andrew grew older and once again, restless.

At seventeen, Andrew decided to enlist as a soldier. Holland was involved in a war in Indonesia and he thought this would satisfy his craving for adventure. After three years of horror and despair, his adventure was cut short by a bullet through his ankle. Thinking he would never walk again, he lay in his hospital bed depressed and confused. He began writing to friends back home and was urged to seek his answers in the Bible. That's when Andrew's real adventure began.

Follow Brother Andrew as he learns to discern and obey the will of God. He first had to learn to walk by faith in all things. When he was ready, God revealed the next step of his journey by sending him to a youth rally behind the Iron Curtain in Poland. Here Andrew witnesses the communist oppression of the church. He sees the hunger for God's Word and determines to return with Bibles and Christian literature. The only way to accomplish this was to become God's smuggler. Again and again he prays the smuggler's prayer: "Lord, in my luggage I have Scripture that I want to take to Your children across this border. When You were on earth, You made blind eyes see. Now, I pray, make seeing eyes blind. Do not let the guards see those things You do not want them to see."

The excitement builds chapter by chapter in this true story of courage and daring where real people risk their lives and freedom to bring encouragement to their Christian brothers and sisters living behind the Iron Curtain.

Vocabulary

Find the word in its context. Reread the sentences before and after the word. What do you think the word means? Look up the word in the dictionary and write a clear, simple definition, and use it in a sentence.

1. bazaar - (pg. 27)

2. coronation - (pg. 59)

3. vagabond - (pg. 63)

4. persecution - (pg. 102)

5. counterfeit - (pg. 123)

Complete the sentences with the correct vocabulary word. OR Write your own sentences using the vocabulary words.

6. The queen's _____ is to begin at 8:00 in the morning.

7. His humble origins and his rebellious nature led him into the life of a _____.

8. The police officer took one look at Greta's I.D. and knew at once that it was a _____.

9. Walking through a _____ in Tashkent, I experienced a beautiful array of colors, smells, and sounds.

10. The young man's new found zeal for God led him into some times of _____ from his former friends.

1. an outdoor market of shops
2. the ceremony of crowning a sovereign
3. a tramp
4. the state of afflicting injury or distress for religious reasons
5. not authentic

6. coronation

7. vagabond

8. counterfeit

9. bazaar

10. persecution

Activities

The following exercises are intended to help you understand and, in a small way, experience the world of Brother Andrew as God's Smuggler. Choose one or two of the following activities. Complete them on a separate piece of paper.

1. Map study: Make a list of the places Brother Andrew mentions, starting with his hometown of Witte. Find them on a map.

2. Interview missionaries about some of their experiences, such as how they received their call to be a missionary, how they knew where they were to go, how God provided for them, and the way they saw God work while on the field.

3. *Eric Liddell* is a biography, while *God's Smuggler* is an autobiography. A biography is written in the third person, and an autobiography is written in the first person. Write about something that has happened to you or that you have done. Write the account as if it were part of a biography and then rewrite it as if were part of your autobiography.

4. Brother Andrew was a faith missionary. That is, he chose to wait upon God to supply all his needs, without letting his needs be known. Perhaps the most famous faith missionary was George Mueller. Read a biography about George Mueller. Check your library.

5. Write a persuasive paper about faith missions. (Refer to Lesson 29 on Persuasive Writing.) You may defend the practice or take another view.

6. Corrie ten Boom was another famous Hollander who lived at the same time as Brother Andrew. Read about her life in her autobiography *The Hiding Place*.

7. While in Rumania, Brother Andrew met a pastor's wife who said, "We've never been able to write letters, and it's thirteen years since we've received one. It has come to us that we are forgotten, that nobody is thinking of us, nobody knows our need, nobody prays." Begin praying for missionaries around the world.

8. Since the writing of the book, there have been some startling changes in the countries mentioned in *God's Smuggler*. Research the countries of Russia, Germany, and Poland. Do they have religious freedom now?

9. Brother Andrew's life began to change as he read through the Bible. If you have never read through the Bible, you may want to begin now.

10. "My heart was racing. Not with the excitement of the crossing, but with the excitement of having caught such a spectacular glimpse of God at work." Write of a time when you caught a glimpse of God at work.

11. We take our Bibles for granted, but the day may come when ours will be taken away, too. Begin memorizing Scripture, hiding God's Word in your heart. You may want to begin with a Psalm. Begin slowly. Memorizing Scripture becomes easier with practice.

APPENDIX

Glossary

Word Parts Lists

Prefixes

Suffixes

Roots

Commonly Misspelled Words List

Spelling Rules

Capitalization Rules

Enrichment Answers

Comma Rules

Glossary

(Adapted from *American Dictionary of the English Language*, 1828)

anoint - *verb* - 1. to pour oil upon; to smear or rub over with oil or unctuous substances. 2. To consecrate by unction, or the use of oil.

battlement - *noun* - (This is said to have been *bastillement*, from *bastille*, a fortification, from Fr. batir, bastir, to build) an indented parapet, having a series of openings, originally for shooting through; an upper wall.

battlemented - *adjective* - secured by battlements.

brands - *noun* - burning pieces of wood; or sticks or pieces of wood partly burnt, whether burning or after the fire is extinct.

caprice - *noun* - a sudden change of mind without apparent or adequate motive; a sudden change of opinion, or humor; a whim, freak, or particular fancy.

cavalry - *noun* - (Fr. *cavalerie,* from *cavalier*, a horseman, and this for *cheval,* a horse, whence *cavalcade*) a body of military troops on horses.

compassion - *noun* - a suffering with another; painful sympathy; a sensation of sorrow excited by the distress or misfortunes of another; pit; commiseration. Compassion is a mixed passion, compounded of love and sorrow.

democracy - *noun* - (Gr. *demos* - people; *crateo* - to possess, to govern) - government by the people; a form of government, in which the supreme power is lodged in the hands of the people collectively, or in which the people exercise the powers of legislation.

design - *verb* - to purpose or intend.

despitefully - *adverb* - with violent hatred; maliciously; contemptuously.

dismayed - *adjective* - disheartened; deprived of courage.

disposition - *noun* - temperament; habitual inclination or tendency.

dross - *noun* - 1. a waste product taken off molten metal during smelting. 2. Waste matter; refuse; any worthless matter separated from the better part; impure matter.

endeavor - *verb* - to exert physical strength or intellectual power for the accomplishment of an object; to try; to essay; to attempt.

engaged - *adjective* - entered into conflict with.

exceedingly - *adverb* - to a very great degree; in a degree beyond what is usual; greatly; very much.

exulted - *verb* - rejoiced in triumph; rejoiced exceedingly at success or victory; to have been glad above measure; triumphed.

fatigue - *noun* - weariness with bodily labor or mental exertion; lassitude or exhaustion of strength.

feigning - *participle* - imagining; inventing; pretending; making a false show.

flanked - *verb* - bordered; touched; posted on the side.

flourish - *verb* - to thrive; to grow luxuriantly; to increase and enlarge, as a healthy growing plant.

foreboding - *noun* - foretelling: usually something bad.

forsake - *verb* - 1. to quit or leave entirely; to desert; to abandon; to depart from. 2. to abandon; to renounce, to reject. 3. in *Scripture*, God *forsakes* his people, when He withdraws his aid, or the light of his countenance.

garret - *noun* - that part of a house which is on the upper floor, immediately under the roof.

honesty - *noun* - fairness; candor; truth.

immortal - *adjective* - 1. having no principle of alteration or corruption; exempt from death; having life or being that shall never end. 2. never ending; everlasting; continual.

impatiently - *adverb* - with uneasiness or restlessness; not patiently.

inaccessible - *adjective* - 1. not able to be reached. 2. not able to be obtained. 3. not able to be approached.

intrigues - *noun* - a plot or scheme of a complicated nature, intended to effect some purpose by secret artifices. The word is usually applied to affairs of love or of government.

mentality - *noun* - mental capacity or endowment; intellectuality; mind.

moldering - *adjective* - turning to dust; crumbling; wasting away.

obliterated - *adjective* - effaced; erased; worn out; destroyed.

olfactories - *noun* - olfactory (pertaining to smelling; having the sense of smell) organs.

omnipotent - *adjective* - 1. almighty; possessing unlimited power; all powerful.

opine - *verb* - to think; to suppose.

perilous - *adjective* - dangerous.

persecute - *verb* - to pursue in a manner to injure, vex or afflict; to harass with unjust punishment or penalties for supposed offenses; to inflict pain from hatred or malignity.

posture - *noun* - situation; condition; particular sate with regard to something else; state; condition.

provision - *noun* - supplies of food; all manner of eatables for man and beast.

prudence - *noun* - cautious practical wisdom; good judgment; discretion.

ramparts - *noun* - embankments.

realism - *noun* - the tendency to view or represent things as they really are.

repining - *verb* - fretting or feeling discontent or of murmuring.

repose - *noun* - a lying at rest; sleep; quiet; rest of mind; tranquillity; freedom from uneasiness.

resolve - *noun* - fixed purpose of mind; settled determination; resolution.

ruddy - *adjective* - of a red color; of a lively flesh color, or the color of the human skin in high health.

sluggard - *noun* - a person habitually lazy, idle and inactive; a drone.

sustenance - *noun* - 1. support; maintenance; subsistence. 2. that which supports life; food; victuals; provisions.

triumphantly - *adverb* - 1. in a triumphant manner; with the joy and exultation that proceeds from victory or success. 2. victoriously; with success.

vagabond - *noun* - a vagrant; one who wanders from town to town or place to place, having no certain dwelling, or not abiding in it.

WORD PARTS LISTS

Prefixes

Prefixes	Meanings	Examples
a, an	not, without	atypical, atheism
ad	to, towards	admit, advance
amphi	both	amphibious
ante	before	antebellum, antecedent
anti	against	antisocial
apo	from, off	apology
be	on, away	bestow
bene, bon	well	benefit
bi	both, twice	bicycle, biweekly
by	side, close, near	bystander, byline
cata	down, against	catapult, catalog
circum	around	circumference
co, com	together, with	copilot
de	from, down	depress
di	two, twice	dissect
dia	through, between	dialogue
dis, des	apart, away, reverse	dismiss
em, en	in, into	embrace
ex	out	expel
extra, extro	beyond, outside	extraordinary, extrovert
fore	before in time	foretell, forefather
hyper	over, above	hyperactive
hypo	under	hypodermic
il, ir, in, im	not	illegal, immoral
inter	between	interrupt
intra	within	intramural
mis	incorrect, bad	misprint
mono	one	monotone
multi	many	multiply
non	not	nonsense
ob, of	towards, against	obstruct, offend
para	beside, almost	parallel
per	throughout, completely	perfect
post	after	postscript
pre	before	premonition
pro	for, forward, in favor of	progress, pro-life
re	back, again	revoke, return
sub	under	submarine
super	above, over, more	supernatural
trans	across, beyond	transfusion
tri	three	triangle
un	not	unfair

213

Suffixes

Suffixes	Meanings	Examples
able, ible	able, can do	predictable, possible
age	state of, act of, collection of	storage, salvage
ar, er, or	one who, that which	governor, teacher
ard, art	one who	drunkard
ary, ery, ory	of, relating to, or connected with	dictionary budgetary, archery
ate	cause, make	segregate
cian	having a certain skill or art	musician
cide	kill	homicide
en	made of, make	wooden
esque	like	picturesque
ess	female	lioness
et, ette	a small one, group	midget, luncheonette
fic	making, causing	scientific
ful	full of	grateful
fy	make	terrify
hood	order, condition	manhood
ic	like, being	scenic
ile	of, relating to, or capable of	juvenile
ion, sion, tion	act of, state of, result of	action
ism	doctrine, characteristic	Communism
ity	state of, quality	captivity
ive	causing, making	exhaustive
less	without	hopeless
ly	like, manner of	princely
ment	act of, state of, result	banishment
ness	state of	happiness
ology	study, science	biology
ous	full of	spacious
ship	office, state, skill	professorship
ward	in the direction of	homeward
y	characterized by	muddy, funny

214

Roots

Roots	Meanings	Examples
am, amor	love, liking	amiable
anthrop	man	anthropology
arch	chief, first, rule	archaic, monarch
aud, aus	hear	audition
auto, aut	self	automatic
bio	life	biology
cap, cip, cept	take	capture, perceptive
carn	flesh	incarnate
ce, ceed, cede	move, yield, go, surrender	recede, proceed
chrom	color	monochromatic
chron	time	chronological
clam, claim	cry out	exclaim
corp	body	corporation
crat	rule, strength	bureaucrat
crea	create	creature
cycl, cyclo	wheel, circular	bicycle, cyclone
deca	ten	decade
dem	people	democracy, pandemonium
dent, dont	tooth	dentist, denture
derm	skin	dermatology
dic, dict	say, speak	dictaphone
fac, fact, fic, fect	do, make	manufacture
fin	end, ended, finished	finale
form	shape	uniform
fort, forc	strong	fortress, force
fract, frag	break	fracture, fragment
gen	birth, race, produce	Genesis
geo	earth	geology
gest	carry, bear	suggest
grad, gress	step, go	gradual, transgress
graph, gram	write, written	telegram, autograph
hema, hemo	blood	hemorrhage
homo	same	homonym
hydr	water	dehydrate, hydrophobia
ject	throw	reject
leg	law	legislature
letter, lit, liter	letters	literary
lic, licit	permit	license
loc, loco	place	locale

Roots	Meanings	Examples
log, logo, ology	word, study, speech	logo, logical
luc, lum, lus, lun	light	luminous
man	hand	manual
medi	half, middle, between	Mediterranean, mediate
mega	great	megaphone
mem	remember	commemorate
meter	measure	thermometer
micro	small	microscopic
mit, miss	send	transmit, missionary
mori, mort, mors	mortal, death	immortal
morph	form	metamorphosis
multi	many, much	multiply
numer	number	numerous
omni	all, every	omniscient
ortho	straight, correct	orthodontist
pan	all	pantheist
path, pathy	feeling, suffering	sympathy
ped, pod	foot	pedestrian
pedo	child	pediatrician
pend, pens, pond	hang, weigh	pendulum, ponder
phil	love	Philadelphia
phobia	fear	claustrophobia
phone	sound	phonics
photo	light	photograph
poli	city	metropolitan
poly	many	polygamy
pon, pos,	place, put	proponent, pound, dispose, compound
port	carry	import
potent	power	potent, omnipotent
prim, prime	first	primitive
proto	first	prototype
psych	mind, soul	psychology
ri, ridi, risi	laughter	ridiculous, derisive
rupt	break	interrupt
sci	know	omniscient
scope	see, watch	microscope
scrib, script	write	transcribe, Scriptures
sed, sess, sid	sit	sedentary, possess
sent, sens	feel	sentiment, sense

Roots	**Meanings**	**Examples**
serv	save, serve	servant, service
sist, sta, stit, stet	stand	persistence, substitute
solus	alone	solitary
solv, solu	loosen	dissolve
soph	wise	philosopher
spec	look	inspect
sphere	ball	hemisphere
spir	breath	Spirit
spond, spons	pledge, answer	sponsor
string, strict	draw, tight	constrict, restrict
stru, struct	build	construction
tact	touch	contact
tele	far	telegraph
tain	hold	contain
tend	stretch	extend
terra	earth	terrestrial
theo	God, a god	theology
therm	heat	thermos
thesis	place, put	hypothesis
tort	twist	controt
tox	poison	toxic
tract	draw, pull	distract
uni	one	unicorn
ven, vent	come	intervene, invent
ver, veri	true	verify
vert, vers	turn	revert
vid, vis	see	television
vita, viv	life	vitamin, vivid
voc	call	vocation
zo	animal	zoology

Commonly Misspelled Words List

1. absence
2. accidentally
3. accommodate
4. ache
5. achievement
6. acquaintance
7. acquire
8. advantageous
9. aggressive
10. allegiance
11. amateur
12. among
13. analyses
14. analyze
15. angel
16. angle
17. apparatus
18. apparent
19. appearance
20. approach
21. ascend
22. athlete
23. attendance
24. author
25. auxiliary
26. beggar
27. beginning
28. believe
29. beneficial
30. benefited
31. boundary
32. business
33. campaign
34. category
35. ceiling
36. challenge
37. characteristic
38. column
39. committee
40. comparative

41. conceivable
42. condemn
43. conscience
44. conscientious
45. conscious
46. controversies
47. convenience
48. criticism
49. curriculum
50. cylinder
51. decision
52. dependent
53. descendant
54. description
55. desirable
56. desperate
57. difference
58. disappearance
59. disappointment
60. disastrous
61. discipline
62. dissatisfied
63. doubtful
64. efficient
65. eligible
66. embarrassment
67. entertainment
68. environment
69. essential
70. exaggerate
71. exceed
72. excitable
73. exhaustion
74. existence
75. experiences
76. explanation
77. exquisite
78. extraordinary
79. extremely
80. familiar

81. fascinate
82. February
83. financially
84. fluorescent
85. forfeit
86. forty
87. fourth
88. fulfill
89. further
90. gauge
91. government
92. grammar
93. guarantee
94. guidance
95. happiness
96. height
97. hindrance
98. humorous
99. hygiene
100. hypocrisy
101. imagination
102. immediately
103. incidentally
104. independent
105. indispensable
106. influential
107. intelligence
108. interest
109. interpretation
110. irresistible
111. involve
112. jeopardize
113. judgment
114. knowledge
115. laboratory
116. leisure
117. license
118. loneliness
119. magnificence
120. maintenance

121. maneuver	148. possessive	175. seize
122. marriage	149. possible	176. sense
123. mathematics	150. precede	177. separate
124. miscellaneous	151. preferred	178. sergeant
125. mischievous	152. prejudice	179. significance
126. necessary	153. prevalent	180. similar
127. ninety	154. principal	181. simultaneous
128. nuisance	155. principle	182. strenuous
129. obstacle	156. privilege	183. studying
130. occasion	157. proceed	184. subtle
131. occurrence	158. professor	185. succeed
132. omitted	159. prominent	186. summarize
133. optimism	160. psychology	187. syllable
134. original	161. pursue	188. temperament
135. parallel	162. quantity	189. tendencies
136. paralysis	163. recognize	190. tentative
137. parliament	164. recommend	191. thorough
138. pastime	165. referring	192. tragedy
139. patience	166. reign	193. transcend
140. peaceable	167. reminiscent	194. transferred
141. permanent	168. repetition	195. vacuum
142. permissible	169. resistance	196. vengeance
143. persistence	170. response	197. villain
144. perseverance	171. restaurant	198. weird
145. physician	172. rhythm	199. writing
146. pleasant	173. ridiculous	200. yacht
147. pneumonia	174. schedule	

Spelling Rules

1. When **ie** makes a long **e** sound, write **i** before **e**, except after **c**.
   Ex: believe, yield
   Exceptions: either, neither, seize, leisure, weird

2. When **ie** does not make a long **e** sound, write **e** before **i**.
   When **ie** makes a long a sound, write **e** before **i**.
   Ex: eight, foreign
   Exceptions: friend, mischief, patience

3. The spelling of the base word does not change when a prefix is added to a word.
   Ex: mis + spell = misspell, il + legal = illegal

4. When a suffix is added to a word ending in a consonant and **y**, the final **y** is usually changed to **i** before adding a suffix. When the suffix is **-ing**, the **y** does not change.
   Ex: happy + ness = happiness
       cry + ing = crying

5. Words ending in **e** keep the final **e** when adding a suffix beginning with a consonant.
   Ex: care + ful = careful
       state + ment = statement
   Exceptions: true - truly, argue - argument, judge - judgment

6. Most words that end in **e** drop the final **e** when adding a suffix beginning with a vowel.
   Ex: live + ing = living, love + able = lovable
   Exceptions: Words ending in **-ce** and **-ge** usually keep the silent **e** when the suffix begins with **a** or **o** in order to keep the soft sound of the final consonant.
   Ex: notice + able = noticeable

7. For words ending in **ie**, change **ie** to **y** when adding the suffix **-ing**.
   Ex: die + ing = dying, lie + ing = lying

8. With one-syllable words ending in a single consonant preceded by a single vowel or words that end with an accented syllable, double the consonant before adding **-ing**, **-ed**, or **-er**.
   Ex: sit + ing = sitting, begin + er = beginner

9. With one-syllable words ending in a single consonant *not* preceded by a single vowel, do not double the consonant before adding **-ing**, **-ed**, or **-er**.
   Ex: seat + ing = seating, leap +ing = leaping

10. Only one word in English ends in **-sede**: supersede. Only three words end in **-ceed**: exceed, proceed, and succeed. All other words of similar sound end in **-cede**.
    Ex: recede, concede, precede, intercede, etc.

Capitalization Rules

1. Capitalize all proper nouns.
   Person's name, companies, trade names - John Williams, Sears, Toyota
   Days and months - Monday, February (not the seasons)
   Special days, events, periods - Hanukkah, Dark Ages, Battle of Bunker Hill, Civil War
   Titles of people - King Charles, Queen Elizabeth, President (when referring to a particular president)
   Planets, countries, streets, etc. - Mars, Afghanistan, Oak Street Pacific Ocean, Pine Street,
   Mt. McKinley, Lake Erie

2. Capitalize the first word in every sentence.

3. Capitalize words like *aunt* and *professor* if it used as a title preceding the person's name.
   Ex: I am looking forward to seeing *Aunt* Jo.
   I am looking forward to seeing my *aunt*.

4. Capitalize words like *mom* and *dad* if they take the place of a proper noun.
   Ex: I hope *Mom* will like her present. (*Mom* may be replaced by *Mary*.)
   I hope my *mom* will like her present. (*Mom* may not be replaced by *Mary* — I hope
   my Mary will like her present — it sounds awkward.)

5. Capitalize nouns, pronouns, and adjectives referring to God and the Bible.
   Ex: Lord, Lamb of God, Word of God, His love

6. Capitalize the names of a particular course.
   Ex: I enrolled for *History 101*.
   I enrolled in a *history* class.

7. Capitalize directional words only when they are used as proper nouns.
   Ex: Magnolias are a beautiful sight in the *South*.
   I have never been *south* of Kansas.

8. Capitalize all proper adjectives. A proper adjective is an adjective formed from a proper noun.
   Ex: America - *American* flag
   Buddha - *Buddhist* monk
   Chinese - *Chinese* food

9. Capitalize titles of books, poetry, movies, etc. Capitalize the first word and every
   other important word.
   Ex: *Anne of Green Gables* - book
   "All Things Bright and Beautiful" - poem
   Star Wars - movie

10. Capitalize the first word of a direct quotation unless it is the first word in the second
    part of a split quotation.
    Ex: "*It's* so good to see you," said Chad.
    "*Hello,*" said Chad, "*it's* so good to see you."

Comma Rules

1. Use commas to separate words and groups of words in a sentence.
   Ex: The fruit salad contained oranges, bananas, kiwi, and strawberries. (separates words)
   Jerry saved up enough money by mowing the grass, raking the leaves, and hauling the trash. (separates groups of words)

2. Use commas to separate two independent clauses when joined by a coordinating conjunction.
   Ex: Janet went to England, and Josh went to Greece.
   (The comma separates two independent clauses. *Janet went to England* and *Josh went to Greece* can stand alone.)

3. Use commas to separate a subordinate clause from the independent clause which follows it.
   Ex: When Janet went to England, she visited the castles of her dreams.

4. Use commas to separate two or more adjectives.
   Ex: The lovely, fragrant flowers filled the room with joy.

   Note: Do not use commas to separate adjectives which do not modify equally (such as numbers).
   Ex: The three little pigs devised a plan to outwit the nasty wolf.

   You would not use a comma between *three* and *little*. They do not equally modify. If you are not sure if the adjectives equally modify, ask yourself the following questions:
   a. If I switch the order of the adjectives, will the sentence still make sense? If it makes sense, the adjectives equally modify. If it doesn't make sense, the adjectives do not equally modify.
   b. If I insert *and* between the adjectives, will the sentence still make sense? If it makes sense, the adjectives equally modify. If it doesn't make sense, the adjectives do not equally modify.

5. Use commas to separate a word or words in a direct address, or vocative.
   Ex: I'll see you later, Jim.
   Jim, I'll see you later.
   Later today, Jim, I'd like to see you.

6. Use a comma to separate a mild interjection from the rest of the sentence.
   Ex: Hey, did you see the game last night?

   Note: An exclamation mark may be used with a strong interjection.
   Ex: Wow! Last night's game was exciting.

7. Use a comma after an introductory or transitional word.
   Ex: Finally, the wedding day had arrived.

8. Use commas to separate a parenthetical phrase from the rest of the sentence. A parenthetical phrase is a word or phrase, when omitted or placed elsewhere, still makes sense and keeps the meaning of the sentence.
   Ex: As a matter of fact, I will see Bob tomorrow.
        I will see Bob tomorrow, as a matter of fact. (Still makes sense.)
        I will see Bob tomorrow. (Still makes sense.)

9. Use commas to separate an appositive from the rest of the sentence. An appositive is a word(s) which identifies or renames a noun or pronoun.
   Ex: Uncle Ken, *known by his family for his unusual diet,* introduced us to tofu ice cream. It was delicious!

10. Use commas to separate a nonrestrictive phrase or clause from the rest of the sentence. A nonrestrictive phrase or clause is one which, if omitted, does not change the basic meaning of the sentence.
    Ex: Gloria, the girl in my drama class, was given the leading role in the school play.
    The phrase, *the girl in my drama class,* is not essential to the basic meaning of the sentence. If the phrase was omitted, the basic meaning of the sentence would not change.

    Note: Do not confuse a nonrestrictive phrase or clause with a restrictive phrase or clause. A restrictive phrase or clause is one which is necessary to the sentence. Do not use commas to set off a restrictive clause.
    Ex: Children who are ill-mannered are not welcome in the theater.
    The phrase, *who are ill-mannered,* is a restrictive phrase because it is necessary to the basic meaning of the sentence. If the phrase is omitted, the basic meaning of the sentence would change.

11. Use commas after a name before a title is given.
    Ex: Marilyn Topper, M.D.   Samuel Bennett, Ph.D.
         Jay Brown, Jr.   William Sims, Esq.

12. A comma may be used to add clarity in a sentence. Sometimes a sentence may sound confusing if a comma is not used. The use of this comma may go against all comma rules. The author is given license to use the comma to add clarity or to add emphasis.

Enrichment Answers

The Enrichment Activities answers are listed below. Since the Enrichment Activities are not numbered, you can easily locate them by the Lesson number that proceeds it in the *Student Activity Book*. Some of the Enrichment Activities do not have a specific answer. For those, please read the directions in your student's book and evaluate the activity accordingly.

Lesson 1
1. SHOAT   6. CHEATER
2. SUITE   7. TRIPE
3. TIGER   8. SQUIRE
4. HOTEL   9. LEER
5. PRECIOUS

Lesson 2
A. Words found in the puzzle: who whose whom which what this that these
those

B. Answers will vary.

Lesson 3
A. 1. atmosphere; not an extraterrestrial
2. Austria; not an island
3. rib-cage; not an organ
4. hockey; does not use a ball
5. iron; not a precious metal
6. L. M. Alcott; not a male
7. botanist; not a health scientist
8. apricot; not a vegetable

B.   Pliable   Solid
1. clay   dough   wood
2. honey   glass   screw

     Carnivore   Herbivore
3. shark   wolf   goat
4. alligator   deer   giraffe

Lesson 4

1. plant, herb, marjoram
2. athlete, soccer player, goalie
3. Canada, Ontario, Ottawa
4. money, coin, penny
5. food, dessert, ice cream

Lesson 5

A. 1. category
   2. part/whole
   3. synonym
   4. characteristic
   5. part/whole
   6. antonym
   7. antonym
   8. characteristic
   9. part/whole
  10. category

B. 1. degree
   2. function
   3. degree or sequential
   4. sequential
   5. homonym
   6. sequential
   7. function
   8. degree
   9. homonym
  10. degree or sequential

Lesson 6

1. function
2. category
3. homonym
4. function
5. synonym
6. antonym
7. homonym
8. category
9. characteristic
10. degree or sequential
11. antonym
12. part/whole
13. sequential
14. antonymn
15. characteristic

Lesson 7

1. staid
2. befuddle
3. gaggle
4. bamboozle
5. command
6. simple
7. fast
8. rode
9. college
10. lamp

Lesson 10

1. sleep
2. hat
3. stationery
4. ballad
5. entertain
6. educate
7. eye
8. air
9. spring
10. state

Lesson 11

Possible answers:

1. quit
2. run
3. location
4. tail
5. fast
6. year
7. thyme
8. look
9. instructor
10. compute
11. attack
12. reign
13. injury
14. many
15. weight
16. strong
17. insect
18. cry
19. liquid
20. learning

Lesson 12

Answers will vary.

Lesson 13

Answers will vary.

Lesson 14

A. Words in the puzzle: aboard against beneath but inside near since through toward within

B. Possible answers:

1. explanation
2. accustomed
3. fiddle
4. homeless
5. affront
6. wiggle
7. follow
8. manner
9. motor
10. ripple
11. preferred
12. disease
13. bottle

Lesson 15

Answers will vary.

Lesson 16

1. Spain
2. Germany
3. Japan
4. Egypt
5. India
6. Switzerland
7. Morocco
8. Australia

Lesson 19

Possible answers:

1. hour
2. moon
3. down   town
4. hound sound
5. tooth booth
6. bored
7. sublime
8. quick coma

Lesson 20
1. 4 seasons in a year
2. 8 notes in an octave
3. 11 players on a football team
4. 30 days in June
5. 12 months in a year
6. 360 degrees in a circle
7. 5 fingers on a hand
8. 3 singers in a trio
9. 2 children in twins

Lesson 21
1. place to keep money   land on a river
2. jewelry   sound
3. type of preserve   congestion of traffic
4. a tool   past tense of *see*
5. type of dog   slang for *food*
6. type of feathers   opposite of *up*

Lesson 22
1. random access memory
2. cash on delivery
3. missing in action
4. Internal Revenue Service
5. self-contained underwater breathing apparatus
6. tender loving care
7. American Association of Retired Persons
8. very important person

Lesson 24
A. Answers will vary.

B. 1. B   2. W   3. Q   4. D   5. G   6. I

Lesson 25
Possible answers:
1. cross boss   5. pink drink
2. witty kitty   6. pale male
3. funny bunny   7. fat hat
4. light bite   8. loud cloud

Lesson 32
    A. Pictures will vary.
    B. Possible answers:

1. critic	8. noon
2. dumped	9. peep
3. entrée	10. rider
4. going	11. systems
5. high	12. toughest
6. kick	13. willow
7. mainstream	14. yearly

    C. Possible answers: dialogue, auctioned, unquestionable, overhauling, encouraging, cautioned, equation, ultraviolet

    D. Answers will vary.

Lesson 33
    Answers will vary.

Lesson 34
    A. Answers will vary.
    B. Answers will vary.

Skills Index

The numbers listed after each skill refer to the Lesson number. The asterisk (*) denotes that the skill is covered throughout the program.

Composition

Grammar

Higher Order Thinking Skills

drawing a diagram - 14
memorization - 6,7,11,19

Student Activity Book Enrichment Activities

Reading

alliteration - 19
anapestic - 19
assonance - 19
autobiography - 35-36
biography - 23,24,35-36
cliche - 13
comparing - 10
consonance - 19
context clues - *
dactylic - 19
dialogue - 15
fiction - 25
figurative language - 13
foot - 19
historical fiction - 16
iambic - 19

literature appreciation - 3
metaphor - 13
meter - 19,33,34
moral - 20
narration - 15
nonfiction - 25
poetry appreciation - 13,19,33,34
prefix - 2
prose - 13,33
rhyme scheme - 13,19,33,34
riddle poem - 34
roots - 2
simile - 13,34
suffix - 2
trochaic - 19
vocabulary - *

Research and Study Skills

concordance - 23
dictionary - *
encyclopedia - 1,6,12,16,25
interviewing - 15

note taking - 25
research - 1,7,8,9,12,17,18
revision - 7
thesaurus - 6,10,11,15

Spelling

Spelling guidelines - 1

Spelling words - *

Additional Books

Books Used in the Book Studies

Aldrich, Bess Streeter. *A Lantern in Her Hand.* New York: Penguin Group, 1983.

Andrew, Brother with John and Elizabeth Sherrill. *God's Smuggler.* New York: Penguin Group, 1967.

Hunt, Irene. *Across Five Aprils.* Follett Publishing Co., 1964.

Swift, Catherine. *Eric Liddell.* Minneapolis: Bethany House Publishers, 1990.

www.commonsensepress.com

Congratulations,

You Are Part Of The *Common Sense Press* Family.

Now you can receive our FREE e-mail newsletter, containing:

- Teaching Tips
- Product Announcements
- Helpful Hints from Veteran Homeschoolers
- & Much More!

*Please take a moment to register with us
by photocopying or tearing out this page and mailing it to:*

Common Sense Press
Product Registration
P.O. Box 5863
Hollywood, FL 33083

Or, better yet, register online at
www.commonsensepress.com/register.

After registering, search our site for teaching tips, product information, and ways to get more from your *Common Sense Press* purchase.

Your Name _____

Your E-Mail Address _____

Your Address _____

City _____ State _____ Zip _____

Product Purchased _____

From What Company Did You Purchase This Product? _____

_____

Get involved with the *Common Sense Press* community.
Visit our web site often to contribute your ideas, read what others
are doing teaching their children, see new teaching tips, and more.